PRAISE FOR *PEACEFUL MAMA*

"This book is needed in the hands of any expecting or seasoned mom who is seeking a more peaceful, connected, and compassionate motherhood experience. As more moms find their inner peace by following the framework laid out in this book, our children and families will experience a shift in consciousness that forever changes them. Give this book to any mom you know and be a part of the movement of peaceful mamas creating a more peaceful world."

—Hal Elrod, Author of the #1 Best-Selling Book, *The Miracle Morning*

"*What to Expect When You're Expecting* is like the Bible for new moms, but it doesn't prepare you for motherhood! *Peaceful Mama* helps you understand what mama-hood is really like and the changes we go through mind, body, and soul. It also gives you practical tools to help mamas find their new normal with MAMAHH Moments. I wish I'd had this book when I was pregnant!"

—Lindsay McCarthy, Co-Author of *The Miracle Morning for Parents and Families: How to Bring Out The Best in Your KIDS and Your SELF*

"*Peaceful Mama* combines practical parenting advice with being-in-the-moment wisdom for Mamas-in-waiting as well as Mamas-in-training. The authors share heartfelt stories of the ways their own children were great trainers for them in the ability to instill openness to surprise and spontaneity! Six MAMAHH Moments capture the essence of the everyday self-compassion and child-centered compassion needed for healthy family life. Each Mama can learn to accept her emotional stretch marks, along with her physical stretch marks, through the peaceful modeling of positive parenting moves in this timely book."

—Janis Clark Johnston, Ed.D., Family Psychologist and Author of *It Takes a Child to Raise a Parent: Stories of Evolving Child and Parent Development,* and *Midlife Maze: A Map to Recovery and Rediscovery after Loss*

"With a kind, wise, and heart-centered approach, *Peaceful Mama* makes it easy for any mom to thrive and create a peaceful, connected, and compassionate environment for her family. This is a book I wish existed when my kids were little. It's a game changer!"

—Patricia Barros, MD, PCI Certified P

"Imagine flowing through your day in a peaceful, centered way, while feeling good about yourself as a person and as a parent. Impossible? That's what this book can give you. Here's a secret: Kids learn from who we are, so becoming the best version of yourself teaches them to do the same. Isn't this really what great parenting is all about? This book will teach you how. As new parents, we become all-consumed with our children while our own needs often take a back-seat. Lindsay and Natalie provide practical solutions for taking care of ourselves so we can take the best care possible of our children. *Peaceful Mama: The Mind, Body and Baby Connection* is loaded with creative and practical ways to be the best parent possible and enjoy the journey!"

—Jacqueline Kelm, Author of *The Joy of Appreciative Living*

"Wow—fabulous book! This book offers the reader raw, insightful, and honest ways to deeply connect with our uniqueness—our mind, body, and soul—and nurture these parts of ourselves that will help us live in flow with peace, and harmony as we share and spread this to our children and the world at large. The reader will gain a deeper understanding of the world of self-discovery and have more tools and techniques as they move forward in raising a family."

—Sue DeCaro, Co-Founder, Building Connected Communities, PCI Certified Parent Coach®

"*Peaceful Mama* is full of the deep feminine wisdom women are craving. We want to be reminded that we can be our own health gurus, that our bodies house powerful creative forces, and that we already have everything we need to feel peaceful and confident through the magical process of creating new life. This book has everything from sensible, down-to-earth practices to insights from experts in the field to profound philosophical food for thought. It's a book all women, not just those that are mamas or pregnant, can benefit from."

—Clara Wisner, Certified Nutrition Therapy Practitioner, *Revolutionary Lifestyle*

"As a physician assistant in women's health, I love the beautiful message and guidance that this book provides. A reminder of the proverbial 'stop and smell the roses.' Life goes fast . . . it's good to remember to breathe and enjoy the ride. Energy, strength, and rebooting one's soul is essential for all earth mamas out there."

—Ashley Meyers Harwyn, PA in Women's Health

"As a Mama, chiropractor and health restoration coach, I believe this book bridges a gap often overlooked in motherhood literature. Valuable techniques of career success are beautifully combined with mom-wisdom shared in a personal and applicable way with a purpose of help long us be better at our most important responsibility: Mama. The way we 'Mama' influences generations—the wisdom in these pages, if applied, will ensure being the best version of Mama a Mama can be."

—Kimberly Minick, DC

"As a women's health educator and hormone balancing chef, I often see women—especially modern mamas—in total burnout. This book is a fabulous resource with a plethora of tools to help keep Mama centered, driven, and full of love as she juggles her many roles of being a woman in these modern times. Not yet a Mama myself, this book was also preparation for me for those exciting days to come."

—Allie McFee, *Modern Goddess Lifestyle*

"*Peaceful Mama* is our modern day conscious parenting manifesto! With useful tools it is a clear and compassionate guide to conscious motherhood, parenting and mindful living through joy, patience, love and intention. As a holistic doula, I am grateful and excited to pass along this book and all the support, guidance and wisdom it provides!"

—Jennifer Radnay, Holistic Doula, Prenatal Yoga and Pregnancy Coach

"As I read *Peaceful Mama*, it was like a soothing, calming salve was poured over my entire being. So simple, yet so deeply powerful! I wish I could give every Mama this priceless education in parenting with grace."

—Rose Cole, Medicine Woman and *Rituality* Founder

"As a conscious motherhood coach and peaceful parent myself, the message of this book resonated with me deeply. In sharing their personal stories so generously, the authors speak for so many mothers with similar experiences and give a voice to those who feel voiceless, isolated, and overwhelmed. This book provides a simple framework mothers can use to invite more compassion into their day and shift their experience of motherhood."

—Catarina Andrade, MSc, CHHC, Energy Therapist for Mothers

"As a chiropractor who works closely with new mamas, I know this book provides an avenue that most are longing for. The reader will learn to become a more conscious, mindful, and present parent. It offers realistic steps to transition your thoughts and actions throughout your motherhood journey to become the best you, which provides the greatest foundation for your kids. Every Mama needs this book on her bedside table!"

—Hayley Miller, DC

"As a mom, this is the book I wish I had from day one! I didn't understand mindfulness until fairly recently and I have become a better mom (and person) because I intentionally practice being present. I also could have benefited from the authors' advice about practicing self-care. This book gives us the ultimate guidance on self-care. . . . Read it and share with every Mama you know."

—Bri P, Certified Health Coach, RN, and Hippie Dippie Mom

"*Peaceful Mama* helps to bring an awareness practice to life. This book is full of simple, practical exercises that you can integrate into your daily life immediately. Mindset is our fourth pillar at BIRTHFIT so this book speaks to our hearts."

—Lindsey Mathews, DC, BIRTHFIT Founder and CEO

"This is a great read and actually exactly what I needed right now! Between balancing a lovable and energetic four-year-old with my (nursing) and newly mobile nine-month-old, not to mention our dog, travel agency, husband and more, I've got a lot on my plate. . . . I look forward to using MAMAHH Moments as daily practices."

—Randee Shyer, Mom, Artist, and Owner of Jetsetting Families Travel Agency

"The majesty of wisdom comes through on every page in this parenting book. This resource validates that being a mother is not a linear path and provides ingenious ways to navigate your way through the unexplored territory. I heartily recommend this teaching memoir, rich with practical strategies and poignant anecdotes, to anyone wishing to parent in a deeply meaningful and intentional way."

—Jenna Bayne, Parenting Strategist and Author of the *BayneBooks Series*

PEACEFUL MAMA

The Mind, Body & Baby Connection

THE MANIFESTO OF CONSCIOUS MOTHERHOOD

PEACEFUL MAMA

The Mind, Body & Baby Connection

THE MANIFESTO OF CONSCIOUS MOTHERHOOD

NATALIE SAGER + LINDSAY AMBROSE

CITRINE PUBLISHING
Asheville, NC

Developmental editing, cover design, and interior design: Penelope Love
Copyediting: Fiona Saltmarsh
Cover art: Ryan McCauley
Photos: Sivan Ravit, sivanravit.com (NS); Sabrina Blackney, sabrinaleephotography.com (LA)

Excerpt from The Work by Byron Katie printed with permission from Byron Katie, www.thework.com

Library of Congress Cataloging-in-Publication Data

Sager, Natalie.
Peaceful Mama: The Mind, Body and Baby Connection: The Manifesto of Conscious Motherhood / Natalie Sager and Lindsay Ambrose
Includes bibliographical references.

p. cm.
Paperback ISBN: 978-1-947708-11-2
Digital ISBN: 978-1-947708-66-2
Library of Congress Control Number: 2018942566
10 9 8 7 6 5 4 3 2 1
1st Edition, May 2018

CITRINE PUBLISHING
1141 Tunnel Road, Suite C #19644
Asheville, North Carolina, U.S.A.
(828) 585-7030
Publisher@CitrinePublishing.com
www.CitrinePublishing.com

To my incredibly supportive family for all their love and encouragement as this Modern Hippie Mama discovers the beauty and wonderment of life and all its possibilities.

~Natalie

To my family for giving me the courage to choose to see beauty and love in each new moment.

~Lindsay

TABLE of CONTENTMENT

FOREWORD

BY SKYE DYER

I have been deeply touched by the contents of this book you are about to read. Natalie and Lindsay have written the perfect guide for those entering motherhood or already there.

I am a new mom. As I write this, my son is seven months old. While I was pregnant I was given a lot of advice, some wanted, some not. Overall it was positive, but some was downright awful, which I'm sure you can all attest to. The greatest gift was talking to women about the real changes that occur and how to handle and love ourselves in a delicate way.

We are all unique in our experiences, but having someone to talk to or share their guidance is beyond beneficial.

Almost every book I read gave advice about pregnancy or the birth, but not on how to take care of yourself after. This book offers support for many issues that mothers face after the excitement of the birth dwindles down and real life with your baby begins.

Childbirth and everything that happens after is intense, in the most beautiful way, but you can get lost if you don't find a way to honor yourself. I thought that I was as prepared as you could be to be a mom, but there were still many things that took me by surprise.

I was three weeks early to the day. I was told repeatedly that your first baby is almost always late, so I didn't have a bag packed. I didn't get checked at thirty-six weeks because I thought *why rush it, let's start at thirty-seven weeks.* My son had another idea, he was ready and coming fast. I just made it to the hospital, I was

7 cm when they checked me, there was no time for an epidural, my son came an hour after we checked in. I relied on my breath and thankfully I had my mom by my side who had birthed seven children-naturally (she is truly superwoman). My son came into the world fast and somewhat easy, which describes his personality as well. I am forever grateful for the gift of being his mother.

The first couple of weeks were amazing but also intense. My son was a cluster feeder (which means he left only short time periods between feeds) so I was breast-feeding constantly and I would barely have time to eat, let alone take care of myself. It took me a little while to find the balance of taking care of myself and my son at the same time. That's why this book is so special, it teaches how to honor yourself and how important self care is.

We can only give what we have and if we are depleted, what are we really giving to our children? I hope the words in this book resonate with you as much as they did for me and guide you to be a Peaceful Mama.

Skye Dyer
Singer/Songwriter
Delray Beach, Florida
May 2018

PREFACE

Every woman's journey into motherhood is uniquely hers. From conception to pregnancy, from delivery to the first year and beyond. It is as unique as the children we bring into the world.

Even though our children and our stories are different, we share commonalities that bond and unite us into the Mama Tribe. Motherhood is the ultimate humanizer because there is nothing else that sparks such tremendous joy while at the same time making us feel incredibly overwhelmed as when we become a parent.

We may think an immediate transformation from standard woman to doting and nurturing mother will take place soon after we conceive. However, we are often surprised to realize the transformation into motherhood is neither fast nor automatic. It takes time to discover our way as a Mama. We hope that throughout this book and throughout motherhood, you will discover the Mama you always dreamed of becoming: the one who cannot be found by looking outside yourself, but must come from searching within.

Like our children, we evolve and grow from challenging experiences that force us to rise above the expected into the unexpected. Motherhood is one of these life-transformational experiences that reminds us change is the only constant. Individually and collectively we have the capacity to evolve and grow in monumental ways we could never have imagined. As we dive deeper into our authentic selves, our essence as women, wives and Mamas, life becomes sweeter, more meaningful, and more peaceful.

Meet Natalie Sager

First and foremost, I am a Mama to my precious sons, Jonah and his baby brother, Skye. They are the light of my life and my constant reminders about how miraculous and wonderful the world can be, when we open our hearts. They are my greatest gifts and teach me something new every day. They open my eyes to new possibilities and encourage me to enjoy life to its fullest. They always remind me to stay present and have fun! But, most importantly they have taught me about unconditional love.

I am also blessed and grateful to have my journey man, my soulmate and the love of my life as my forever partner. Thank you, Lance, Sage Abraham, for supporting me, loving me, believing in me and inspiring me to live my true self. I love and honor you.

As the Modern Hippie Mama, I am an author, a speaker, a holistic health promoter, and a meditative Yogini who empowers all beings, especially Mamas, to live in pure health with an abundance of happiness. As the main powerhouses in the home, we can then create a ripple effect to our family, friends, community, and beyond. My dream is to reach as many Mamas across the world as possible so that we can positively shift our mental, physical, and spiritual health for the collective benefit.

Between solving the "mystery of colic" naturally with my first baby and then having a miraculous recovery from severe jaundice with my second baby, I have quite a bit of experience in the roller coaster of emotions a new Mama can go through. In this book, I share those experiences and the lessons I have learned from them with anyone ready to fully embrace health and happiness.

It is my goal to be optimally healthy so I can watch my family grow throughout the years and during that journey I aim to help others find the same light. Simply put, I know that when one Mama shines her light in her family, everyone in the world is positively affected!

MEET LINDSAY AMBROSE

For me, motherhood is about balancing many things through the choices I make each day. It's about finding the flow that works, knowing it looks a little different for every single one of us. It is a blessing to say I feel happy with the balance I have found now, and it's ever-evolving.

Moms would tell me all the time how fast it goes, and to enjoy motherhood because it goes by in a blink. I started to wonder how I could enjoy the days and the moments more so I didn't look back on my motherhood experience the same way. I learned that when we are paying attention to ourselves and filling ourselves up outside of parenting—in our health, work, relationships, emotions, spirit, mind, and heart—then we feel better and can give more to our families. I began to notice a shift in my parenting as I started to prioritize a little time for myself amidst the busy days. I learned there are tools that help, such as mindfulness, which is becoming more aware in a nonjudgmental way and choosing where I focus my attention. I learned that my emotions are energy in motion and are present in every single moment.

As I become more aware and responsible for my own energy, I can choose to take a moment before reacting to what's going on around me and respond with intention. I learned that with greater mindfulness, I can get through the inevitable tough times of parenting with more ease and feel the joy of the good times with greater presence. I felt like I needed to share what I was learning with other moms so we could all appreciate more, worry less, and be here now with our children.

I started a podcast and blog to unite moms by sharing how whether we work inside or outside the home, have one child or six, by being more mindful and intentional and finding fulfillment in our own life, we can make our everyday, fleeting moments with our families more meaningful. I called it *EveryDayEveryMom*. I definitely didn't have it all figured out so I started to interview moms who were finding fulfillment in their days and could share their life recipes with us. I had no idea of all the amazement that would ensue from taking that brave first step of starting *EveryDayEveryMom*.

INTRODUCTION

BY BRAHMANAND DON STAPLETON, PH.D.

As Mother's Day comes again this year, I am filled with gratitude for the space in my heart that has opened as I receive the gift of wisdom embodied in the learning process that is stimulated in this wonderful book by Natalie Sager and Lindsay Ambrose.

I recently met Natalie in a retreat that focused on deepening the capacity to make choices that empower us as individuals to establish a more loving interior communication between the many layers of our conscious awareness. In such a workshop, the surprising "aha" moments center around confronting the reality that there are many unconscious layers within oneself that have been inaccessible in one's inner world. What excites me about the messages in this book (which is not just for mothers, by the way) is receiving and digesting a treasure chest of exercises and daily practices that nurture the ability to use my own intentionality to love myself as the inner being who longs for and deserves to give myself to the world surrounding me. One of these lessons is described so simply by Lindsay:

> "I began to notice a shift in my parenting as I started to prioritize a little time for myself amidst the busy days. I learned there are tools that help, such as mindfulness, which is becoming more aware in a nonjudgmental way and choosing where I focus my attention. I learned that my emotions are energy in motion and are present in every single moment. As I become more aware and responsible for my own energy, I can choose to take a moment before reacting to what's going on around me and respond with intention."

As I make the space in my life to listen more deeply to the love a Mother gives and receives in her life role as Mom, I could not feel more trusting of the voices they bring into the conversation of cultivating the capacity to generate deeper love from within myself. And how great it is as a man to nurture my strength and vulnerability to awakening the wisdom that comes through the midwives, doulas, naturopaths, homeopaths, acupuncturists, counselors, coaches and other holistic health care professionals that Natalie and Lindsay bring into the conversation about how we all can bring peace, happiness and greater fulfillment into all of the roles we fulfill in life.

When I wrote *Self-Awakening Yoga: The Expansion of Consciousness Through the Body's Own Wisdom*, I opened many doorways to generating deeper confidence in listening to the voice of our own inner wisdom for loving guidance. The knowledge shared in *Peaceful Mama* has carried me to an even deeper understanding of the limitless capacity we all have to express our true Self. As Natalie says, "I know that when one Mama shines her light in her family, everyone in the world is positively affected."

Thank you, Natalie Sager and Lindsay Ambrose, for paving the road for all of us in ways we could never have imagined.

Brahmanand Don Stapleton, Ph.D.
Co-Founder and Co-Director of Self-Awakening Yoga
Nosara, Costa Rica
May 2018

PEACEFUL MAMA

The Mind, Body & Baby Connection

THE MANIFESTO OF CONSCIOUS MOTHERHOOD

Chapter 1

Our Stories

Natalie

One moment you are going about your daily life and in the blink of an eye everything can change. Your world can completely flip upside down. That's what happened to me with both my children.

My pregnancy with Jonah was rather delightful. I was able to teach (and do) ballet barre and Pilates until the day my water broke, literally. I had the typical morning sickness first trimester, felt amazing second trimester, and started to become very uncomfortable further into my third trimester. I was not as Modern Hippie Mama as I am now, so there were some distinct differences in my choices for prenatal care and delivery.

For example, I had an OB instead of a midwife, and nurses instead of a doula, and a hospital instead of a nice warm tub in my home. With that being said, my OB was a lovely woman and Mama herself and I adored her. She was supportive of my birth plan, which was basically that I intended on having a vaginal delivery with an epidural, no synthetic hormones, no forceps, etc. My "plan" was for as natural a delivery as possible while still being medicated. I look back and laugh at that now because I have changed so much. But, at that time, those were my wishes and it is what I believed I could handle. That being said, I pretty much had the most textbook hospital birth ever.

When my water broke at home, hubby and I were in such a state of excitement and frenzy that we both stopped, looked at each other, and said, "What do we wear to the hospital?!" It was so funny! We were about to completely change our lives and welcome a little baby into the world and our first thought was *what do we wear?* That was the first of many questions we would be faced with that day.

Once we had gotten to the hospital and checked in, we were given a room to settle into. After a couple of hours, the nurse came in and asked how I was doing. I said that I'd honestly had no pain and I was just waiting for the fun to begin. Then my OB came to check on me and said she wanted to give me Pitocin because I was not "progressing" fast enough. In my heart I did not want to take it. I had been warned against taking it as it can encourage potential complications. Unfortunately, I did not follow my intuition and she proceeded to give it to me. Fortunately, I began contractions pretty shortly thereafter. I requested the epidural and was disappointed when only half my lower body felt the effects. I was none too pleased, but I was at least grateful for some relief.

"How you feel today may be different tomorrow or with future pregnancies. A piece of advice I can stand behind is this: gather information, ask your heart what resonates with you, be open to hearing new thoughts and ideas you may not have considered before, and trust in the process."

~ Natalie

After several hours of labor, I was finally ready to push. Lance was holding one leg, a nurse was holding the other and my OB was the catcher. When Jonah Myles made his appearance, the doc said, "I have never seen that much hair before!" We were laughing so hard. And, of course, I was immediately asked if I had heartburn during my pregnancy as this is an old wives' tale suggesting the baby has a lot of hair. He was born with a full head of hair and a cute, little mohawk. He was absolutely adorable and I felt so relieved to hear him crying. The nurses immediately laid him on my chest and after he nursed for a bit, the nurses took him to get weighed and measured and to run some tests on him.

Lance went to keep hawk eyes on Jonah while he was with the nurses. I felt the epidural and Pitocin still racing through my blood. I was shivering one minute and crying the next. I was not sure if I was going to throw up or pass out. I felt overwhelmed, anxious and uneasy in my own skin, and I did not like it at all. I remember wondering if the way I was feeling was normal or if there was something terribly wrong. I was able to finally calm myself down after several hours. But, I was still not feeling like myself.

I distinctly remember thinking about all the women I knew who had given birth and wanted so badly to know how their experiences were during labor, delivery and postpartum. I couldn't imagine that my emotional and physical state were average. My mind started to become fearful and it was in this moment that I wondered if I had made the right choice (for me) to have an epidural and be convinced of the Pitocin. And, I made sure to commit those feelings to memory for next pregnancy.

I also clearly remember thinking to myself, *"Holy what the hell did we just do?? Are we even ready to be parents?"* And, then I judged myself for having that thought and immediately convinced myself I shouldn't have those thoughts or feelings because everybody knows when you give birth you are supposed to immediately feel like life is filled with roses and butterflies. And I did not. So, within the first few hours of being a Mama I was already feeling like a failure.

Jonah had high bilirubin levels and was experiencing jaundice. The hospital let us go home but only if we promised to bring him to the pediatrician first thing the following morning. We did and when we got there the pediatrician said his levels were still high. We needed to monitor him, keep him in the sun, count his wet diapers, and come back the next day. I was terrified. She had explained to us what could happen and the severity of the situation. I was already a hot mess and this added stress was the opposite of helpful. Fortunately, when we brought him the second day, his levels were going down and we could finally breathe a little more deeply. Thank goodness!!! Now, I would be completely lying if I said the rest of our experience with Jonah as a baby was only delightful. It was a challenge for us. But, more on that later.

What I will say is this: you and your husband/wife/partner will evolve and change as the years go by and your priorities and values may shift and change. So, how you feel today may be different tomorrow or with future pregnancies. A piece of advice I can stand behind is this: gather information, ask your heart what resonates with you, be open to hearing new thoughts and ideas you may not have considered before, and trust in the process. The experiences and situations I shared with Jonah were stockpiled in my head for pregnancy number two. Consider being a nonjudgmental collector of information as you open your eyes and mind to new possibilities in your Mama journey.

I had the most wonderful pregnancy with my second child, Skye. Sure, I had a little sciatica, but for the most part I felt pretty fabulous. We decided to have a home birth. (Well, our baby decided for us that he wanted to be born at home so he guided us along that path until we committed!) It was our little secret. We didn't want anyone's fears projected on us, so we kept it between us, our midwife and our doula. And, since this Modern Hippie Mama is a water girl, I wanted to labor and deliver in a birth pool.

If you know me personally, you know I am a planner. I like every detail thought out thoroughly. When our midwife did her home visit and we showed her our "supplies," she couldn't believe how prepared we were. From Chux pads to a water filter, underwater speakers for personalized sound therapy, waterproof chakra lighting, birth affirmation scrolls (courtesy of my amazing hubby), a birth flag created by my friends and moms at my baby blessing, Himalayan salt lamps, and candles—and what birth would be complete without some sage burning? We had it all. Now, everything just had to go according to plan...

And, it did. I know you were expecting a twist, but not yet.

When I gave birth to Skye, I was filled with a pretty deep and complex range of emotions. We had an absolutely amazing birth. It was a raw, insanely animalistic (I literally roared like a lioness several times during labor), totally intense, life-changing and deeply empowering event.

To be honest, there were a few times during labor that I did not think I could go on. At one point, I was moaning, "I can't do this." And, my amazing doula was encouraging me and reminding me that this was "the plan," "MY plan," and I remember shouting in response, "Bad plan!" But, I was already committed and needed to birth this baby!

I can giggle about that now, but I can also tell you that the experience I had was completely transformational for me. When baby Skye was born, I could not believe I had accomplished the Herculean task of childbirth sans medication. But, that was what Skye wanted. That's why, while in utero, he gently nudged and coaxed and finally convinced me to commit to a home birth. So, I acquiesced and followed his lead.

But, when Skye entered the world, it was no longer about me. Our lives changed forever. Skye Alexander, our full-moon baby, had a beautiful entrance into the world and two great days at home.

After the initial high and complete disbelief of what my body, mind and spirit allowed me to do, I realized I needed time to actually process what had happened. Like, time to sit and talk to someone about my experience and get feedback and hear about their personal and professional experiences with childbirth. Was mine "normal" or "typical" or "textbook"? Who knew? All I knew was that I had this delicious little boy who needed me. I also had a physical, mental and emotional body that needed healing and love. And, to boot, hormones attempting to balance themselves out.

Day three postpartum, I was nursing baby Skye when I looked into his eyes and said, *hmm, he's quite yellow.* And, then I took him outside and instead of the *hmmm*, I said, "Holy shit, this boy is bright yellow!" So, I called the pediatrician (who, side note, had seen him and given him the thumbs up the day he was born, as hours after delivery we took him to the ped's office for an evaluation.)

When I told them I was concerned about his bilirubin levels, the doctor's office told us to come in ASAP. When we arrived the nurse took one look at baby Skye and said, "Wow, he's glowing!" She ran to get the doctor and sent us to the hospital "stat."

From there, the nurse poked his little foot and started squeezing blood out. After what seemed like twenty minutes of torturing our son, she was finally done and sent the blood to the lab. They came back and told us they didn't get enough blood. "Not enough blood?! They took two vials! Make it work! I don't want him to go through that again!" The doctor called us while we were in the waiting room and I just looked at Lance while he was on the phone. I saw him bow his head slightly and close his eyes in fear. My heart dropped. *What had happened?!*

After that, things are kind of a blur. They rushed us to the ER where we were surrounded by nurses and doctors. They were telling us that his bilirubin levels were off the charts: 25 is severely high and Skye was at a 32.5. They took his blood again and it spiked to 35.7. The doctor was telling us he was going to "throw the kitchen sink" at baby Skye. "What?! No. Let's slow down here. We don't want antibiotics. A blood transfusion? What are you talking about?" And, then they whisked him away.

Lance and I stood there looking at each other. *How did this happen? What is going on? This is* not *our life!*

We had done everything in our power to stay out of the hospital and here we were. This was not a part of my plan. My illusion of control was ripped out from under me. And, my son's fate was in someone else's hands. NICU doctors and nurses who didn't know me or my family, or understand our values or desires, were in charge of my baby's well-being now. For all I knew, they just viewed my precious boy as another patient.

But, they saved him. With compassion and love and kindness. He had eight nurses and two doctors work with him and every single one of them was an earth angel. The NICU team referred to him as a miracle baby because they had never seen numbers that high and he broke a record at the hospital. They never lost faith, and they gave us hope with every update.

At three days old, they had to do a full blood transfusion and give him antibiotics, IV fluids, two rounds of IVIG, a CT scan of his brain and spine, and an IV through his belly button. He was in intensive care for five days and his levels finally dropped. It was an extremely difficult and emotional week.

Lance and I are non-traditionalists and naturalists when it comes to medicine and healing. We believe the body can heal itself with proper nutrition, lifestyle, environmental, emotional, and spiritual connection. But, we also believe there is a time and place for Western medicine. This was the time and place and we are forever grateful. As with everything we preach, it is not just one thing that saved baby Skye—it was a combination of things. Because we are truly blessed with friends who are faith healers, bio-magnetic healers, sound therapy healers, energy healers, etc., we were able to surround Skye with what he needed to heal. By the grace of God, prayer, family, friends and much healing, loving energy, he is strong and healthy now.

I was certain that *the* question on everyone's mind was: would this have happened had we done a hospital birth? That was my first fear also. But, my midwife, doula and the NICU doctors all agreed it was not because of the home birth. It was because Lance and I have two different blood types. And he is also Coombs positive, which makes a baby susceptible to anemia and jaundice. All of this was out of my control and not preventable. Jaundice spikes on the third day of life, so even if I'd had him in the hospital they would have sent me home by then. And knowing me

I would have requested to go home after twenty-four hours anyway. If we decide to have another baby I will do a homebirth again, but this time I will have them immediately check the blood type and determine whether the baby is Coombs positive. I strongly believe that having a homebirth helped him. If we had been in the hospital, there would have been interventions that would have made him weak. But he was so strong going into the hospital that it helped save his life.

My little warrior, Skye, is here to change the world. He already has. He reminded me that life can change in an instant. That life is a gift and it is our obligation to ourselves to enjoy the moment, love our life, and find happiness in every situation.

Now, the lessons he taught me and continues to teach me were and still are only able to become clear to me after having some sleep, proper nutrition, meditation and visualizations.

When you have an infant and a young child, sometimes sneaking in all of those self-care acts can be challenging. Fortunately, when Skye was about six months old, we (hubs and I) stumbled upon *The Miracle Morning* by Hal Elrod. We both listened to the audiobook since we had limited opportunity to sit and actually read a book. But, we were grateful that we made time to listen to his story, his journey, his suggestions, and his solutions. All completely valid, honest, helpful and manageable.

However, trying to do all of those every day as a new Mama sounded challenging and slightly unrealistic. But, Lance and I decided to give it a try. The thought of getting less sleep than I already was with an infant struck me as far from appealing. But I was determined to make a positive impact on the world and I knew, deep down, that the only way to make that happen was to begin within myself.

In a nutshell and according to Hal himself, *The Miracle Morning* "is an instructional book all about how to create a morning routine that sets you up for success in every aspect of life. Now practiced by thousands of people worldwide, The Miracle Morning is helping transform lives and create greater success for its readers. By using the morning to invest in and develop yourself, you too can live the Miracle Morning and start on your path to success."

However, that change was not going to happen during baby-waking, Stay-at-Home Mama hours. It needed to happen during my "off time," hahaha. I know. Mamas are always Mamas and never get to "call out" of being a Mama. But, there are some opportunities for nourishing our souls, and that's what needed to happen because a happy and healthy Mama means a happy and healthy home.

By way of the Universe, I found out that Hal and his team were planning to do a Mastermind event in Chicago a few months later. There was something inside of me urging me to go. Like a little tap on the shoulder nudging me, saying "Natalie, you need to attend this." So, I (somehow) convinced Lance that I needed to attend this event.

And, I am so grateful that I did! Not only was the event filled with incredible value and content galore, but the high energy and the amazing people I met were totally priceless. This is where I met Lindsay Ambrose, Mama of three, *EveryDayEveryMom* podcast hostess and blogger. We were partners during one of the improv exercises and although we didn't majorly succeed on our assigned task, we did laugh a lot and connect on a personal and professional level. Our missions were in direct alignment with each other and our personal goals of helping Mamas was clear.

After the event, Lindsay and I stayed connected and she asked if she could interview me for her podcast. Of course, I was honored to be featured and was super excited to share my story and hopefully connect with and help some of her listeners through my experiences. Isn't that how we all learn, after all? Through experiences? Whether our own or from those of others? Anyway, we got to chatting and agreed that we had something special that we wanted to share with the world.

So, we joined forces and created this handy manual for Preconception, Prenatal, and First Year Mamas. After reading several books on pregnancy, childbirth, parenting, etc., we felt that there was still something missing. There's an aspect of new Mamahood that has been overlooked, or not talked about, swept under the rug as seemingly unimportant. It's the amazing roller coaster of emotions you go through; it's the questions you ask yourself but are hesitant to ask someone else, it's the golden opportunities we have throughout the day and throughout our journey as Mamas. It's the idea, hope and possibility that there is so much more available to you—as a woman, a warrior, a wife, a daughter, a sister, a friend and a Mama.

It is our hope to provide you with the tools to ignite your inner fire and trust that you are chosen to be right here and right now, to fundamentally shift you and your family's life. When one person shines their light on the world, everyone is positively affected. With the love, support and encouragement of fellow Mamas, I am confident that we can collectively create a ripple effect to change the world.

Lindsay

I didn't realize how different every pregnancy, birth, and child-raising experience was until I experienced it myself. I see firsthand how each of my pregnancies, births, and children are so monumentally unique. The moment I let go of fear and worry and judgment, I began to trust myself and my inner ability to parent my children in the best way for them. That was the moment motherhood became everything I hoped it would be. I still worry and lose faith at times, but now I have tools in my belt to bring me back. When I'm practicing awareness and mindfulness and really being present with my children, I am my best. I am the best I can be for my children. That's when being a Mama just flows and I am learning and growing myself and Mamahood becomes sweeter every day.

Being a mother is something that was just inside me. I'd always wanted it. When my husband proposed to me, one of the first thoughts I had after saying "yes" was *now we can have children.*

I found out I was pregnant on the morning of my twenty-ninth birthday. The overwhelming feeling of excitement I felt the moment I saw that positive pregnancy stick is truly beyond words. I was amazed by all the changes my body made as I grew this new life inside me. I was so in awe with what was going on inside that I truly had that pregnancy glow outside.

Pregnancy gave me a new outlook. I loved what being pregnant sparked within me. I had a strong desire to eat well, knowing I was nourishing this miraculous being growing in my belly. I wanted to work on myself, our home, anything to make it better for this child who would enter our lives. I read a lot. I wrote about what I was feeling. In my efforts to be better, I spent a lot of time looking outside to find something that would and could only come from looking inside. Of course, I didn't realize it at the time

My son came into the world in late November 2011. The first feelings I had about parenting were that it was the most challenging yet beautifully amazing and wonderful thing I have experienced in my entire life. That remains true today. I have not encountered anything else that both challenges yet beautifies my world in the way parenting does.

My labor with my son was nothing I expected or planned. Two days after my due date, my water broke. Without any contractions prior to that, they started immediately and grew strong quickly.

Labor moved along swiftly from that point. It was intense beyond words and I eventually had an epidural that eased and calmed me. However, just as swiftly as the labor came on, it came to an abrupt stop just as I was supposed to be nearly done. The nurses kept asking, "Do you feel that desire to push?" I was 9 centimeters dilated but the feeling to push never came. I guess he was stuck a bit, being face up, as they said. So after trying many different things, the best choice was to have a C-section.

I was heartbroken. After many hours of labor, all I wanted was to experience the birth I always thought I would have, as my mom did, and her mom before that. I had never even considered having a C-section.

At this point of tiredness and exhaustion, I sensed urgency from the doctors, who moved forward and fast. It was an emergency C-section. I signed the waivers and before I knew it I was in the operating room. My husband, Dan, stood next to me in scrubs with a mask on. It was scary, overwhelming and intimidating. I didn't like it at all. At one point, I was so upset from the tiredness and disappointment and worry that I couldn't calm myself. The doctor said close your eyes and that really helped. The brightness of the operating room and all the machines and people working on my body went away in that moment. What felt like only moments later and a lot of pressure, I heard the beautiful, shrieking cries of our son. I opened my eyes and felt ease and total joy.

It was *the* most amazing low and high of my life. My doctor remarked, "It's a boy and he's a jumbo baby." They put him next to me and I was so in love.

He was our perfect ten, 10 pounds, 0 ounces. We named him Calvin.

I didn't feel my tiredness from being up for countless hours. I didn't feel discomfort from laboring and then being cut open. It was the first of many times during motherhood that love took over and brought me energy I didn't know I had.

When they finally placed him in my arms and we headed to the recovery room. It was a feeling I truly cannot even put into words except to say, it was a miracle. As he latched on and I fed him for the first time, it felt like the most amazing accomplishment of my life.

"I have not encountered anything else that both challenges yet beautifies my world in the way parenting does."

~ Lindsay

I was so happy. Over the next few weeks as my body was healing, we were simultaneously learning to care for an infant. It was difficult, to say the least. The recovery from surgery was painful and it took a while to feel good in my body. But it was also so beautiful and wonderful. His little noises. His soft skin. His bright eyes. The way he nestled into me to nurse and slept so peacefully on me. I reflect back on those first few days of Calvin's life and smile remembering that it was the most challenging, wonderful, amazing experience of my life and is still.

The first few months with Calvin were hard. He wasn't a peaceful, calm baby. Since he was my first, I just thought this is how babies were. He cried a lot. I exclusively breastfed him but it was often a struggle of having enough milk. It seemed he wanted to eat and eat but after he ate, so often he would feel discomfort. I couldn't console him and I felt completely helpless and overwhelmed at times.

But there was a major change after Calvin's first two months. It was as if his body finally caught up and he didn't feel whatever it was that made him so uncomfortable for those first initial weeks. He felt happier and smiled often. He had grown into that bright-eyed, loving baby boy I saw glimpses of in those first months.

After a three-month maternity leave, I knew I needed to return to work. The decision was heartbreaking for me. I was someone who wanted to stay home but I knew I needed to work for a bit so we could build the life we wanted for Calvin and our family.

We found a wonderful daycare for Calvin while we worked and saved money, and soon enough our dream of having our second child and buying a new home had both become realities. We left our condo in the city for a home in the suburbs as a family of three with one on the way and we were excited about where we were headed. I'd been blessed with another wonderful pregnancy. No sickness, just a lot of joy and excitement and anticipation of this new little person who would join our already sweet life.

My husband and I made the tough choice to have another C-section, as the doctors recommended. It felt like the right one. The other option would have been a vaginal birth after Cesarean section (VBAC—"vee-back"—for short). Knowing what I know now, I'm not sure I would have made the same decision of choosing a repeat C-section over a VBAC. Now a VBAC is not for everyone. There are specific reasons why women need to have C-Sections. However, I was someone who was a candidate for the VBAC. I was consumed in fear of what could have happened, afraid that vaginal labor wouldn't work again and I would be in the same situation of having a long, complicated labor followed by a C-section. I was afraid of the uncertainty, unpredictability, the pain, you name it. There is always something to fear, it's up to us to choose love and trust instead moment-to-moment. I know now that a right decision for me can only come from me. It comes from within. Yet, I didn't have the tools then that I have now to tune in and listen to that still, quiet voice within, that guides each of us along our own unique path. I felt within me that I wanted to try to deliver vaginally. My heart felt like the baby wouldn't be as big and that I could do it. I didn't listen to that voice. I listened to the doctors and lost that chance of delivering naturally. It's hard to look back with regret since I was blessed with a beautiful, healthy baby and uncomplicated delivery. I don't know what could have happened.

I learned two big lessons from that experience. First, when it comes to my health, I have to be my own advocate, trusting myself and my body—something I have to do for myself and will have to do for my children until they too can do it for themselves. Second, that it's good to get second and third opinions. I could have explored other doctors' offices that do more VBACs. They are out there and I just wasn't aware of them at the time. I didn't and in the end I'm the one who lives with the decision. It was up to me to stand up for myself. I made the best decision I could at the time, but next time I will remember to listen to the voice within and be courageous enough to trust it, knowing I have to create space in my life to listen.

However, I did rely on the second tremendous thing I learned from my son's birth: that we aren't in control as parents (and humans) and change is the only constant. Children are their own beings, starting in pregnancy and becoming very apparent in birth. We have to allow the experience because we don't know the birth we will be dealt, just as we don't know who our child will be. Their dreams, passions, drive...it's their story, not ours. We have to surrender to that and just be present and loving and not lose ourselves in it. Each child is their own self and will be who they are destined to be.

We may try to fight that by embedding our own dreams and story for them but that only makes our parenting journey harder. We have to let go of our control and embrace the change. The experience will be greater than we could have imagined as long as we release our own expectations and trust in something greater that will grow us and our children in ways far beyond those that our reasoning, logical minds could ever see.

So on October 2, 2013, we headed to the hospital in a very different way. We were familiar with where we were. We were showered and fresh as we calmly walked through all the steps of the miraculous impending birth. It was still terrifying but not in the same way as before. I trusted the process and couldn't wait to meet the little baby that had been growing so beautifully inside me over the past months.

I held Dan's hand and felt the familiar, immense pressure as a team of doctors and nurses did what they needed to do to take life from inside of me and bring it into the outside world. Pure joy again when I heard the sound of that little, fierce cry as the doctor said, "You don't have one of these. It's a girl."

She was healthy and rosy and beautiful! The same overwhelming feelings of joy and accomplishment and gratefulness flooded into me as they placed her in my arms. As she latched on and fed for the first time, I was so in love and so very grateful.

I used to not understand how you could share your love when you have a second child. I know now your amount of love just grows. The more we give, the more we get back and that's how it was when Lucy came home.

We named her Lucy Mae but nicknamed her "Sweet Lucy Mae" because that is what she was. She cried when she was hungry. I fed her and then she was calm and sweet again. It had been so different with Calvin. She didn't have the same incomprehensible discomfort and irritation that Cal seemed to have at times. She was a baby and had her moments, but no more than would be expected.

It was such a contrast from the first months with our firstborn. Lucy's mostly calm state made the transition into having two so smooth. So smooth that I was ready to do it again much sooner than I was after having Calvin.

At home with them now, I was just so happy. It felt so good to be there with them. Even though it was also a lot of work caring for two children under three, I took it all in stride. It enlivened me. My experience working while I had Calvin helped me feel more grateful for my time at home now. The moments of total joy helped me forget about the tough moments. There was so much joy.

It was the end of spring and we were outside again, enjoying our time together as a growing family. My husband and I talked about having our third. It was soon but we were ready, and baby Paige was ready too because we got pregnant right after we made that decision. This time I *knew* the symptoms I was feeling. So when I picked up that pregnancy test, I already knew the answer. I still can't even comprehend the joy of seeing that third positive pregnancy stick. We were beyond thrilled again.

I felt the early pregnancy tiredness a bit more as I was home with two young children and didn't get the rest I got in my first pregnancies. But my children continued to enliven me with their pure presence and love and energy. Gratefully and successfully, we made it through another pregnancy and delivery.

Several things happened around the time I got pregnant with Paige. I started working again part-time for my former employer. It felt like I had reached the perfect balance. I was working about ten hours a week—mostly from home making my own hours, which gave me some "me-time"—while spending the rest of the time at home with my children.

A few months into this ideal situation, I started to feel that pull of something inside me telling me I needed something more. It was around this time I decided to embark on a personal development experience called Lifebook. A friend recommended it to me as life-changing and it was truly. I went in December of 2014. I was seven months pregnant and overall really happy with where I was in life at that time.

The experience of looking at my life over the course of the three-day event was truly amazing. Their process has you assess your level of fulfillment across all twelve areas of life—health and fitness, intellectual, emotional, character, spiritual, love relationship, parenting, social life, career, financial, quality of life, and life vision—and then it guides you through visualizations, videos, and conversations to write about where you are now and where you want to be.

So I set goals, visualized where I was heading, and learned a methodology to move toward my ideal life vision. It was then that I uncovered my true passion for both motherhood and writing. These are the things that fill me up. Not too long after that experience, I started a blog where I would write about my motherhood experiences called *EveryDayEveryMom*. I didn't know what exactly it would be like or where it would go but it felt like the right step.

I liked where I was in life as we approached the end of my pregnancy. I still kept up the part-time work, but finally I was working on something else for myself that felt so fulfilling and right for me. In light of my newfound creative expression, I stood in a centered and grounded place when we welcomed our third child into the world.

We had another C-section planned for the afternoon of February 13, 2015. I had a wonderful morning with Cal and Lucy at one of our favorite places, the Garfield Conservatory in Chicago. We explored and had a fun morning together, so similar to ones we've had before but different because I knew it would be the last outing with just the three of us. After lunch, the children headed to the grandparents' and we headed to the hospital to meet our new baby.

Even though I *knew* what to expect, I felt the exact same nervousness and excitement as if it was my first while they made all the preparations for surgery. The roller coaster of emotions was no different. We waited for the sound of that sweet cry and as we heard it, the overwhelming feelings of joy flooded in again. It was just as sweet and unexpected and beautiful as with Calvin and Lucy. It is such a joyous miracle to bring a child into the world and I am still amazed and unnerved by it.

The transition with Paige was hard, as you try to give your all to your older children while still keeping up with all the feeding and nurturing of your little baby. It takes a lot out of you but the moments of joy and love and quiet with your little one make it all worth it.

I tried to accept whatever help was offered to me and asked for help when I needed it. I relied on my husband and he really stepped up around the house in those first trying weeks. I felt grateful for friends and family who dropped off meals. That is the other neat thing about having your second or third: your community has grown and you have so much support. It could be a warm meal, a pick-up from school, or a playdate. It all helps so much and there is so much for which to be grateful.

I learned by this time how crucial it is in those early months to take care of myself. I learned it the hard way, not really allowing for that time with the other two, but finally learning to prioritize care for myself helped me transition faster and smoother to life with three children. When Paige started sleeping for longer stretches, I prioritized quality time for myself and could give more to my parenting.

My "me-time" has always been early in the morning. Not an easy time to take when you are up all night with a newborn. But once I started getting those longer stretches of sleep and felt like I could wake up a little earlier than my children, I did and it made all the difference.

Not too long after I started that early routine for myself where I would read and go for a run and do some writing, the same friend who recommended I go on Lifebook gave me a book called *The Miracle Morning* by Hal Elrod. She said it too was life-changing and she was accomplishing more than ever since reading and applying it. I was intrigued and devoured it right away. Elrod's framework for a morning practice that includes silence, affirmations, visualizations, exercise, reading, and scribing (writing) was exactly what I needed to formalize my practice and maximize my results. I was waking up early almost every morning—of course three children under five got in the way of it at times—but I had more energy than I thought could be possible. I was achieving goals that I had laid out for myself when I wrote my Lifebook.

Fast forward another year from then to the summer of 2016. I am still practicing the Miracle Morning. I had left my part-time gig to focus my free time on *EveryDayEveryMom* and now I'm blogging regularly, podcasting, and thinking about writing a book—I was in a really good place.

When I saw that that the author of *The Miracle Morning* was planning a mastermind event in Chicago, I was intrigued. I felt a little nudge from that voice within telling me I should go. I reached out to my friend who had recommended Lifebook and *The Miracle Morning* and it turned out she was attending the event and she offered me a guest pass. I knew I couldn't pass up the opportunity.

With three young children who rely on me heavily, it wasn't easy to make plans to be away from them for three full days. But I remembered how transformative it was in my life to get away and make time for personal development when I attended Lifebook—so I made it happen.

The event truly was transformative. Taking time away from the busyness of our everyday to find more clarity with my life vision is something I had vowed to make a priority. Not only that, the room was filled with really amazing people. I got to connect and learn from other attendees who were doing such wonderful things. It was inspiring and I felt honored to simply be in the presence of people who were living so brightly and on purpose.

And as you now know, this is where I met my co-author, Natalie Sager, a fellow Mama following her own passion for educating and inspiring Mamas through the journey of Mamahood. I was impressed by her energy and passion for her work, and revered the way she talked about the journey of motherhood. I knew right away our paths were destined to connect in some way.

I asked Natalie to be a guest on my podcast, *EveryDayEveryMom*, where I interview moms who are finding fulfillment in their lives and making everyday moments with their children more meaningful by filling themselves up as people first. It was so clear that she was up to something really amazing and I wanted to learn more.

We connected a few other times throughout the event but then left and went on doing the things we do, still inspired and encouraged by the remarkable experiences and conversations we had shared. We scheduled our podcast interview for a few weeks after the event and our conversation flowed effortlessly. It was a wonderful interview and the synergy between our beliefs about motherhood and the spiritual experience of bringing children into the world was so apparent.

We chatted long after the interview, knowing we needed to collaborate in some way. So in this sacred bit of time we'd carved out for ourselves, we set an intention to write about a new way of mothering, one where we see the experience as a way to grow ourselves into new ways of living and being, with more purpose, mindfulness, and love. A way where we are connecting with other Mamas instead of comparing or judging. And through a series of emails and calls, we developed and tested the MAMAHH Moments practice detailed in this book, devoting moments of each day to Movement, Affirmations, Mindfulness, Abundance, Health and Heart.

Natalie and I know that our parenting experiences are as different and unique as our children. It is personal and precious and we are all doing the best we can with the tools available to us (awareness being one of them). Motherhood is a time when we need to support one another by sharing tools and experiences so we can make every day a little better for every mother. Knowing we are all experiencing and feeling the waves of emotions, Natalie and I have created a community for getting it all out and sharing tools for getting through it *all* with more calm, love and joy. Our collective intention is to offer creative ideas for making your motherhood experience one where you grow yourself in ways you didn't know were possible and to be a part of a supportive, welcoming tribe.

Dear Peaceful Mama, may you open yourself up to all the joy, presence and possibilities our children bring. And welcome to the tribe!

Chapter 2

Starting Our Own MAMAHH Moments Practice

Natalie

Waking up early was not a novel concept to me. In fact, when I was a child, my dad would wake me up early in the morning to ask me if I wanted to go work out with him (we had a home gym). Ninety-eight percent of the time, I hopped out of bed and enjoyed some morning exercise before school. Even in elementary school, I quickly felt the benefits of rising early. Some days would be gym days and other days my dad would take me to the ice-skating rink so I could practice figure skating before school.

Looking back, I am first overwhelmingly grateful to my parents for all the incredibly beneficial and lifelong habits they helped me to create. But, also for their unconditional love, support and belief in me that I could accomplish anything I wanted. Writing this now, it reminds me how the confidence they instilled in me is truly a gift that keeps on giving. I hope that I too can impress upon my children the positive core beliefs I first learned from my parents.

Something so seemingly unimportant—waking up early—realistically can have a massive impact on the trajectory of your life...when you have guidelines and a plan. I think that may have been the missing link for me back then. I had a goal: either exercise or practice figure skating. My intention was to feel energized and get my body moving for the day, which inevitably helped to boost endorphins and get the blood flowing to my brain in anticipation of a long day at school. However, the missing link may have been the idea that perhaps it's not just exercising that needs to be done in the morning. Perhaps the key to productivity, positive mindset, fulfillment and enjoyment lies in additional morning practices, as well...

So, fast forward to when I had baby Skye. I led a sleep-deprived existence and was not exactly in my best frame of mind. Not to mention, my mental stability was, frankly, not quite stable as a result of everything we had gone through. The fear of losing your newborn infant haunts you to the core. Long after he was home "safely" in my arms, I still had this sickening, guttural feeling like something else would happen. Like I was waiting for the other shoe to drop. So between my internal distress, my raggedy mental state, and anxious emotional state, I was not exactly skipping through my days. Needless to say, this was affecting my entire household.

When Mama's not healthy, nobody is happy.

As a result of my haze, my hubby was also feeling the downward spiral. He was getting little sleep because our older son was waking up multiple times during the night and Papa was instructed to be with Jonah since I was nursing and could not lend my breasts to my hubs, Lance, to help me. Although, the idea did cross my mind several times. The energy in the house was vibrationally running low and the frequency was continuing to drag us all down. We all needed sleep...but, did we?

Enter *The Miracle Morning*. Both my hubby and I listened to the audiobook and decided we needed a major shift in our lives in order to find happiness and homeostasis in our home again. We craved a routine and a guide to help us reach our long-term goals and get back into the swing of things. What we needed was a good ole kick in the rear and *The Miracle Morning* was just the fire to light under our arses to get us going. So, we committed to practicing the Miracle Morning.

Now, as much as we love Hal, the book, and all its principles, we also had (as previously mentioned) an infant and a three-year-old who were not sleeping or waking at reliable times—a.k.a., we couldn't reasonably or feasibly commit to waking up at a set time every day to achieve the full benefits of the Miracle Morning because we didn't know when the children would wake up. So, we had to tweak things, personalize them, and make them conducive and realistic to our situation.

I was impressed and motivated by the program's Life S.A.V.E.R.S. and the idea of accomplishing each of these morning rituals: Silence, Affirmations, Visualization, Exercise, Reading, and Scribing. The question was, how and when and also which ones were completely non-negotiables for me. So, as a firm believer in the benefits of exercise for whole mind-body health, I committed to taking spin classes at 5:45 a.m. I was on a personal mission to lose the last bit of "baby weight." Although vanity played a part in that desire, it was also driven by the wish to *feel* like myself again. And, with that added weight I did not. I was neither confident nor happy. I felt stuck and totally unsexy. I realized losing the weight wasn't about anyone or anything except me. I wanted to feel amazing and proud and confident and "normal" in my own body again. And, spinning was not only helping me burn calories, but I took the opportunity to majorly multitask. I'm a Mama. That's just what we do.

So, what do I mean by multitasking while spinning? Well, I'm so glad you asked. You know the Life S.A.V.E.R.S. rituals I mentioned? Well, I wanted to combine as many as I could into my time away from home as possible while still honoring the integrity of each. I started visualizing myself at my happy weight. Feeling amazing in that body. There are a few photos of myself that I'd look at and think, *"Yes! That's my body!"* So, as I was spinning, I visualized those pictures in my head. I remembered the bathing suit I was wearing, I remembered how the clothes fit my body, I remembered the confidence and pride I felt. And, as I was spinning, I had my eyes closed and I was feeling those emotions. It was so real I would catch myself smiling. And, then I'd start thinking about how funny I probably looked, sitting on a spin bike with my hair all messy in a morning bun, spinning and sweating my ass off, with my eyes closed and this giant grin spread across my face. I allowed myself to laugh at that image and then brought myself right back to the visualization.

When I became very familiar with this visualization pattern and could get to that meditative state, I started adding in affirmations and "attached" them to the pictures. So, I would visualize the picture of myself in the bikini, the dress, etc., and then I attached a powerful affirmation to it. *"I am confident. I am a Goddess. I am thin. I am lean. I am powerful."* Each of these affirmations was linked and synced to a specific photo. Think of it like a slideshow. Slide one equals pic of me in bikini and I would say one affirmation. Slide two, picture of me in a dress and I would say another affirmation. Slide three, picture of me smiling and I would say a correlating affirmation. Make sense? I was in such a zone that I really had no idea what was going on in the class. Third position, second position, standing, sitting. I really didn't pay much attention to the actual spin class. I called it meditation in motion. I was in the zone and I loved it. These meditation-visualization-affirmation sessions were so powerful that I began losing the unwanted weight, which I was unable to do after my first pregnancy. My mind started to shift and I became happier again, me again, sane again.

> *"One of the biggest lessons I have learned as a Mama (and majorly continue to learn) is to manage my expectations and go with the flow."*
>
> *~Natalie*

The missing pieces for me were the two S's: Silence and Scribing. And, although I was in a total meditative zone while spinning, it wasn't technically silent. So, I started thinking about when and how I could implement that into my day. And, then it occurred to me that I have a ton of time for silence! Hello? I'm a breastfeeding Mama! That means every time I'm nursing my little dude it's another opportunity for silence, connection, appreciation and gratitude. Instead of checking my phone and trying to be "productive" as my angel of love slept on me after he nursed himself to sleep, I decided to use that as an opportunity to enjoy silence. Letting my mind wander and acknowledging those thoughts as they drifted by like clouds in the sky. Or, repeating a mantra over and over again. Sometimes I would just repeat the H'oponopono prayer (I'm sorry, please forgive me, thank you, I love you) with the intention to heal my own body, mind, and spirit as well as my family's.

Nursing has always been sacred to me. It's a time for me to snuggle and love on my baby/toddler. For us to bond in a way that no one else in the whole world ever could or would be able to share with my babes. Providing liquid gold nutrition and nourishment while simultaneously providing warmth, comfort, love and protection. It's pretty amazing, to say the least. And, then I totally elevated the joy by inserting the silence piece. As baby Skye slept and dreamt away, I was able to also dream—a proactive daydream. It was perfect.

The final missing piece was the scribing. I absolutely love writing. I have always loved writing. But, with two young ones and minimal time, it seemed a bit unrealistic for me to be able to sit down and just free write. By the time night rolled around, all I wanted to do after nursing Skye to sleep was crawl into bed. And, my days were filled...so, now I had to get super creative with this one. Thank you, talk-to-text. Greatest invention ever. I decided that the best time for me to "scribe" was post workout when I was still on my meditation-in-motion endorphin high from spinning. I would have these realizations and profound messages come to me while spinning. So, immediately after class when I would go into the locker room, I'd take out my phone and talk-to-text (well, talk into my Notes page on my iPhone and repeat whatever had come to me during that class). They were quick tweetable quotes that were gifted to me from the divine. And, now I could keep track of them in an efficient and usable manner. Genius!

Implementing each of these practices into my everyday had monumentally shifted my own energy which inevitably created a ripple effect unto my family. It. Was. Awesome. It was also a way for me to feel like I had some semblance of control (read illusion of control) over how my day would unfold. I was a much more present Mama. My communication skills with my hubs massively increased and we started to find clarity in what we wanted to do with these precious lives we had in front of us.

Now, full disclosure, there have definitely been times when I was not able to get the full monty of miracle morning practices in because Skye was teething or Jonah was not sleeping well, or my body was speaking to me and telling me to slow down. However, I always took an opportunity to do at least one of the Life S.A.V.E.R.S. on a daily basis. And, the more I was able to do, the better I felt. Over time, I adapted my practice to fit my unique needs as a Mama. Which is why we created MAMAHH Moments.

Lindsay and I decided to write this book to share our own versions of self-care for Mamas and how you can totally personalize these principles to fit your individual situation. When you're a Mama, your "schedule" is constantly changing. Once you get into a routine, someone starts having a growth spurt or needs extra attention, etc. And, as much as I loooove me a schedule, one of the biggest lessons I have learned as a Mama (and majorly continue to learn) is to manage my expectations and go with the flow. Remember though, that:

Little by little, a little becomes a lot.
—Tanzanian Proverb

So, weaving your MAMAHH Moments throughout the day, little by little, you will begin blossoming into a healthier you and a more nourishing lifestyle.

I am a visionary, a planner, a doer. I will push myself to my potential and beyond. Sometimes sacrificing my own well-being. It's both a gift and a curse. Mamahood has helped me tremendously in learning how to slow my roll and rock in flow with the universe.

LINDSAY

Ahhh, the irreplaceable feeling of seeing your baby finally peacefully sleeping after a night of unrest and nursing. You finally lay your head down to sleep and it feels like pure bliss. Then what feels like only moments later, you hear those sounds of your baby stirring again or your other children waking. It's not an easy moment. You want more than anything to sleep, but you know those little ones with sleep in their eyes and huge smiles on their faces are ready to snuggle right into you and you don't want to disappoint them. So you find some energy within you, wake up and greet them with that same smile and open arms they have for you. And it's worth it.

Every morning isn't this extreme, but we face that choice every day. Go back to sleep or wake up.

The decision to rise early, before my family, became much easier once my youngest started sleeping through the night, or at least for longer stretches. When our children are sleeping more, so are we. Trust me, new Mamas. They will sleep. One of the reasons I stay motivated to wake up early is because I am happy about what happens in the early morning—precious, uninterrupted time for me. The only time of my day that is totally for me. It doesn't always happen because of the inevitable child wake-ups, a cough, an early riser or someone who needs some extra comfort. However, waking early has become a habit and I do it most of the time. It's my Miracle Morning and it's made all the difference in becoming a better version of me, day by day.

It started a few months after I had Paige. Cal was three, Lucy one and half, with Paige finally starting to sleep longer stretches, I felt glimpses of myself again. I wasn't in the total sleep-deprived haze anymore. Something amazing happens when your newborn gives you a little more sleep. Thankfully each of my children did it faster than the one who came before. I think it's because we had such a nice routine with the other children that the younger ones seem to fall into it so beautifully. I'm sure that creating and maintaining bedtime routines helped contribute to their mostly reliable sleep habits.

As busy as we are as moms, we start to get really efficient with our time once we see how little we have. So much of your day is consumed in responsibilities for the house, the children, the job, the school and so much more—our time becomes so precious. Finding time in the day for you is not easy but sometimes "the more we have to do the more we end up accomplishing," and that's how it's been for me since having children.

I come from a family of early risers, which may be why it came more easily for me. I loved that my mom was always up before me. Later in life she started running early most mornings. I knew I could do it too. It would have been impossible two months earlier, but I started to feel those glimpses of myself again and I knew I wanted to get my body back and just feel good again.

I started getting up a little earlier to go for a run. It was hard at first, a lot of walking to start. Our bodies change so much through pregnancy, delivery and post-partum recovery, whether from a C-section or vaginal delivery. We have to take it slowly and listen to our bodies.

Waking up and making myself a priority felt *so good!* I've read that exercise activates the same part of the brain that an antidepressant drug does and I believe it. It's an incredible mood shifter and keeps me more centered throughout the day.

My early mornings started as just a few times a week and evolved to my waking up early most mornings. When I didn't jog, I would do some writing and reading and it was so fulfilling. I remember a shift taking place in my overall mood, the way I responded to my children, and my energy level. I had more energy at the end of the days when I exercised than when I didn't. I would nurse my daughter Paige around 5:00 a.m., she would go back to sleep and then I would head out. It was working.

I would try to be home from my runs before my children woke up. But on the occasional morning when they woke up before I returned, my husband really became my partner and advocate. As a mom who exclusively breastfed all the babies, a lot of the night-time work was on me. So having a time for him to step up felt good for all of us, even if it was difficult at first. Aren't all new things difficult, at first? Until you do it a few times. Practice your new practice and then you find a groove. Any change is challenging but once it becomes a habit, it's easier.

Not too long after I started this routine, my friend (someone who says she is absolutely *not* a morning person) shared *The Miracle Morning* book with me. She said she was not only waking earlier than she ever had, but was feeling so great about all she was accomplishing. I already knew the power of the morning, so I was intrigued by the book and found myself immediately drawn into Elrod's story of being in a bad place and how starting these practices changed the trajectory of his life. So he laid out a really practical framework for others to do it too—what a gift!

Like Natalie, I eventually customized my practice into the MAMAHH Moments. We refer to the practice as moment-to-moment because moms rarely get a stretch of time to complete all the practices. As moms, we get a moment here and moment there. But along with my coauthor, I have learned in any moment that I can practice these things, my days are so much better.

Here's how I do it "every morning"—I wrap every morning in air-quotes because that is my intention but it doesn't always happen in full or at the start of my day. With young children, there are disturbances and late nights, making it nearly impossible to do them all at once every morning. Yet even on the really rushed mornings, I can do some variation of this and it always helps me.

MAMAHH MOMENTS: THE BASIC FRAMEWORK

Here I'll introduce the basic fundamentals of the MAMAHH Moments fully detailed in Chapter Six. It's a taste of what's to come, but not a substitute for the later chapter, wherein Natalie and I will help you design and customize your own MAMAHH Moments practice.

M: Movement
A: Affirmations
M: Mindfulness
A: Abundance
H: Health
H: Heart

M – MOVEMENT

I usually go for a run. On the days I don't run, I do some yoga or stretching. I try to get in any kind of movement I can at this time. A run is always great because running is also meditation for me. I have time to think about my affirmations, visualize, listen to a podcast or audio book, and just think clearly and practice mindfulness. As I mentioned earlier, movement in my day has tremendous effects on my mood and energy level. My husband can always tell at the end of the day if I exercised or not. I can be so much more short and irritable, all from not exercising, it's amazing.

Movement is something I teach throughout the day to my children. We walk or ride bikes when possible. We attempt to make the park or play in the yard a daily occurrence. We do yoga or exercises or dancing if the weather or life has kept us inside. Movement raises everyone's moods. It's a go-to for me whenever we need a lift.

A — AFFIRMATIONS

The next part of the practice is affirmations. I keep them on my phone in an app called Trello. I am constantly updating them and revising them as I discover new things or have changes to my goals. I set affirmations across all areas of my life, including personal, parenting, spiritual, career, marriage, wealth, health, organizing, home and more. I incorporate the daily activities and habits I need to do to reach the goals I set. I enjoy reading through these and try to really feel what I am saying. This is the missing link that many people dismiss when practicing affirmations. How does the idea of the affirmation FEEL in your mind, body and soul? Memorize that feeling in your being and the affirmation becomes increasingly and measurably more powerful.

The next part of this I personally really enjoy, and that is the act of visualization. As Natalie described, my visualization is linked with my affirmations. I go from saying the words, to visualizing myself doing the required tasks, to making these dreams a soon-to-be reality. I see myself in the future and also today and tomorrow doing different things that lead to me realizing my ideal life vision. I also have a personalized voice recording, describing my vision. I sometimes listen to that during this time. I also focus on specific things happening later in the day or week that require my focus and attention. I will often visualize my ideal if I feel like I need support in accomplishing something. It's really powerful.

As part of visualization, I also do some meditating at this time. I usually sit in silence for ten minutes using a timer or doing a guided meditation from the app, Insight Timer, which is great. Some meditation sessions are better than others and that's okay. The intention is to *just be* during this time and be intentionally conscious of the present moment, recognizing the thoughts that come up, accepting them, and finding the good in them. It's not easy because I often have so many thoughts that spark emotions, but I just try to bring awareness, acceptance, and kindness to it all. The real benefits of the practice come throughout my day as I'm more aware, centered, and able to find goodness in my experiences.

M — MINDFULNESS

I lie in my bed for a few moments after my alarm goes off and take a few deep breaths, really focusing on the in and out of the breath. I try to just let myself be while being mindful of the moment and think about a few things I feel grateful for. Next I get out of my bed, change into my workout clothes (always right next to bed because I have to set myself up the night before) and slowly head downstairs, hoping not to wake anyone in my family but always peeking my head into their doors and feeling more moments of gratitude for the little ones sleeping peacefully in their beds.

I continue my mindfulness practice as I head downstairs. First I do some reading. I am always in the middle of a couple of books—usually personal development books as I love this genre, but I also read parenting books, memoirs, or my latest book club book at the time. I spend ten to twenty minutes reading.

A – ABUNDANCE

This is an area I'm always working on—abundance comes down to mindset for me. When I can take a few moments to get myself into a mindset of abundance and prosperity, it makes a big difference in my overall well-being and my ability to see things positively.

It's all too easy to get stuck in our heads in a loop of thinking about everything that we lack or that isn't going well. I have to consciously change that mindset. A few moments of focusing on what is going well, and where I am feeling abundance in my life, does the trick! It helps me to remember that the universe doesn't understand the word "can't." If I want to attract more money and save, I need to change my language from "I can't spend money on things that aren't meaningful for me" to *I spend money only on things that bring lasting joy.*

It's easy to pray for abundance but it's essential to watch our words and make sure we aren't inadvertently affirming a lack of it. I approach it like a game, challenging myself to focus on all the areas where I am attracting what I want in my life and use positive language about the areas where I want to make changes. Sometimes even the tiniest focus on our language and the words we use can make a tremendous difference in our own mindset, our level of well-being, and the abundance we are experiencing!

H – HEALTH

I start every morning with a hot mug of lemon water. I remember reading that it is good for your digestive tract and it has just become my routine now. My children are usually rising around now so breakfast always comes next. I've learned the importance of filling my body with good things and how my being healthy affects the rest of the family. I plan our meals as best I can, then fill our pantry and fridge with good food that will help them create healthy habits. I want my children to understand food is our fuel, and to not only know how to make the right food choices but also know how it is prepared. When possible, we cook together. I take them shopping with me and we talk about the food. This is something that we practice throughout the day.

H – HEART

When I practice MAMAHH Moments, I can silence the voices in my head that don't serve me: those little voices that judge, compare and prevent me from living whole-heartedly in this moment and taking in all the love my children are here to share with me. I am also listening to that voice that is guiding me toward a more purposeful, meaningful way of life. Spending more time doing the things I love, that are mean-ingful to me, fills up my bucket. When we are feeling fulfilled, we give more to our families. We give more to them because we are choosing love for ourselves and others throughout the day.

So this is the practice I set out to do every day. In the beginning, I started waking up around 5:30 a.m., an hour before my children usually wake up. Now I usually rise around 4:45 a.m.. It varies day to day but it's amazing how I have shifted my internal clock. I am always amazed at my energy levels from waking up so early. I can accom-plish more when I start the day this way with purpose and in alignment with who I am and how I was designed to live. It is a miracle.

As we carry out these practices throughout the day, we feel so much better at night. Even if I had a crazy-busy day and felt like I didn't have time for any of my MAMAHH Moments, I try to make time for it at night by simply setting my inten-tions for the next day.

Among all the insights gained from *The Miracle Morning*, my biggest aha came when Hal talked about the message we are sending to the universe when we wake up in a negative way, not wanting to rise. When we are hitting snooze and dragging our-selves out, our day starts differently. When we wake up with purpose and positivity, we carry that with us throughout the day. A noticeable shift takes place.

Therefore the last thing I try to do every night before I go to sleep is say my affirmations, the same ones I say in the morning. But at night, I end with an affirm-ation like this:

> *"Thank you for these seven hours of sleep.*
> *My body is amazing and seven hours of sleep*
> *is all I need to rejuvenate and wake up*
> *refreshed and ready to start the day."*

I've read that the last thought we have before bed is often the one with which we wake. When we go to bed thinking we are tired and won't have enough sleep, we often wake up feeling that way. When I choose to think something differently, something positive, I wake up that way. Also, by saying my affirmations, I feel like I am planting positive seeds in my mind that will sprout in me throughout the night. I also try to write out three things I am grateful for, three things I am praying for, and three intentions or goals for the next day. This way I get my worries out of my head and out into the universe. I put my mind to work at night toward waking up with a solution or at least feeling at peace with the unknown of whatever is going on. Essentially I am setting my intention for the next day. I am always amazed at how much more I accomplish when I write out my goal or intention. It's as if the universe works with you when you set your goals and life conspires to help you accomplish them.

The last thing I do as I close my eyes is visualization. I try to visualize myself in the life I dream of from my heart. I focus on different aspects of my ideal life vision and it's a profoundly positive way to end the day. It doesn't happen every night. Sometimes I have fallen asleep in the middle of this process but as I said earlier, I stay flexible. This is my intention. The MAMAHH practice helps me rid myself of guilty feelings and instead find gratitude for the next opportunity to seize that intention. I am grateful because I have seen all the positive effects it has on my life. I see it in my mood, my energy, and in the goals I am reaching every day. I am truly living a better life than I was a few years ago, not to mention reaching goals I never thought would be possible.

Why We Practice MAMAHH

People don't understand how we have time in our days for all that we do, but our secret is pretty simple. Incorporating MAMAHH Moments has such a strong impact on our ability to accomplish more. It lays the framework and creates the vision and practice we need to make these different things happen in our lives, for which we are so grateful.

MAMAHH Moments are a way we can take all of our favorite personal development practices and make it possible for moms to experience peaceful moments throughout the day. Enough peaceful moments strung together makes for a peaceful, happy existence. It's true that a one-hour morning practice isn't realistic with a newborn, but we can still make these practices a part of our day for a few moments, feel the positive effects of them, and expand into the practices as life allows. When we are feeling personally fulfilled, we can give more to our families and make each day more meaningful.

At that time in my life I was not as enlightened with holistic living and nutritional knowledge as I am now, however I had gut feelings about certain things and am thankful I did. I was on birth control pills for many years on and off and decided that it would probably be wise to stop the pill about a year before we started trying. Although, there were many doctors and Google searches that tried to convince me that staying on the pill was "fine." Something inside of me just felt that getting off the pill for an extended time was the best choice for me. Listening to that little voice inside me versus accepting the advice of someone else was one of several times in my life that I am grateful for having adhered to my intuition.

So, while the exact moment when you feel like a Mama will vary greatly from woman to woman, what is scientifically proven is that the mental, physical, emotional, social, and spiritual health of a Mama is vital to the well-being of herself and her baby. As previously stated, I am a planner. I like to have the illusion of control over as many aspects of my life as possible because it brings me a sense of calm. I am not naive, however. I am completely aware that in reality there is very little that we are actually able to control. In fact, some of the simplest yet often most challenging things we do have control over are our responses, reactions, and becoming aware of our mind chatter.

For several reasons, incorporating MAMAHH Moments into your daily life is an important first step whenever possible. And, these can start pre-conception, prenatal or postpartum, and remain a part of your life thereafter. It feels so good to take ownership of the mental, emotional, physical, social, and spiritual dimensions of your life. The first gift is a monumental positive shift in your attitude, which starts with being thankful for your well-being, because as my Mamy, Suzy, always says: "You can do anything as long as you have your health!"

As part of your daily goals, try to be proactive not reactive. Instead of taking care of yourself when you are already unwell, start preparing your mind and body for health so you don't get unwell. Strongly consider investing time, energy, and thoughtfulness into your mental, spiritual and physical health and begin creating wellness in your life.

Wellness is about optimizing your performance and optimizing your life. It is not about avoiding symptoms or pain. It's about getting the best out of your health, the most out of your life, and enhancing your human experience. What's the point in living longer if the quality of life involves medication, pain and suffering? Start practicing the MAMAHH Moments today and you will thank yourself for years to come.

"We are all unique individuals. Even if you could stand in someone else's Mama shoes and experience all that she has in a lifetime, your perceptions would be entirely different."

~ Natalie

MASTER THE MENTAL CONNECTION

Our mental health—which affects us as well as our families and children—is affected by many things. For example, epigenetics is the science of looking "above the genes" to explain changes in gene expression versus considering our genetics a fixed fate. As it turns out, we are the masters of our genetics because we have options and choices. We are in control—once we understand the mental connection to everything.

In light of my own experiences, I am a true believer that we are able to rewrite the future by incorporating healthy practices on a daily basis. MAMAHH Moments allow me to align with my higher self and follow the divine right path for me. With that being said, there are plenty of people who may read that sentence and think "Oh, dear. She's one of those people who believes in woo-woo." And, although I say, "Bring on the woo-woo!" I do understand and respect that everyone may not have the same spiritual belief system. Which is why I like to make sure to have sources from reputable scientists who state that we can, in fact, rewire our brains and therefore affect our offspring.

"Perception is awareness shaped by belief. Beliefs 'control' perception. Rewrite beliefs and you rewrite perception. Rewrite perception and you rewrite genes and behavior...I am free to change how I respond to the world, so as I change the way I see the world I change my genetic expression. We are not victims of our genes. We are masters of our genetics."

—Dr. Bruce Lipton, Cellular Biologist

How's that for grounding out the woo-woo?

Positive thinking can promote healing, but negative thinking is equally as powerful in creating disease and even death. Positive and negative thoughts are profoundly affecting our future. Thoughts give rise to emotions. We have 50 trillion cells in our body and every thought releases different neurohormones. They go into our cell membranes to signal to the brain that you can change the way DNA makes protein. We are made up of over 50 trillion cells. That number is mind-blowing. To put that into perspective: one trillion seconds ago was 32,000 years ago.

We have a magnitude of thoughts every day, thousands and thousands of thoughts. Thoughts translate into chemistry through our nervous system. A thought of love translates in the brain into wonderful hormones like oxytocin and dopamine and suddenly we feel a surge of love and energy. Conversely, stress, *not your genes,* is the greatest cause of cancer and disease in the world. When we learn to see the world differently, we can enjoy a much healthier, happier and more peaceful life.

How often do you walk into a room and immediately begin judging? Whether it's the people, the decor, the culture or yourself. It's almost like your brain is on autopilot. You're thinking, "She's really skinny. She must not eat. I wish I were that thin." Or, "she looks so young, I hope I look that good when I'm her age," or "whoa, look at the size of that...(fill in the blank)." The point is that instead of thinking about what you don't have or what you wish you had or what you used to have, why not be grateful for what you DO have. Be thankful and appreciative for all the blessings you have in front of you. Be loving and kind and gentle to yourself and respect yourself for who you are and what you are. We are so unbelievably fortunate to be here today—alive and capable of personal growth and development. We are so lucky that we woke up today with a strong, beating heart and the motivation to read this book to better ourselves. We can surround ourselves with like-minded people who want the best for themselves and their families and are taking action to make that come to fruition. We manifest our own happiness.

Stress is only stress when we perceive it as stress. For example, we can only be stressed out about the inbox full of emails if we perceive that to be stressful. We are all unique individuals. Even if you could stand in someone else's Mama shoes and experience all that she has in a lifetime, your perceptions would be entirely different.

Remember the 19th century German fairy tale turned 1937 Disney movie, *Snow White?* The Queen looks in the mirror and claims her infamous, "Mirror, mirror on the wall, who's the fairest of them all?" It is a classic example of how your outer world is a reflection of your inner world. When we are full of joy and aliveness on the inside, that is clearly depicted on the outside. Your eyes are the windows to your soul—when you look into someone's eyes you can see deeply into their essence. Are they genuinely happy or are they hurting? Our mental state plays a crucial role in our happiness and when we realize that we have the power to choose happiness—life changes before our eyes. As you read this, remind and ask yourself:

I am here. What is going on inside my body and mind?

EXPLORE THE EMOTIONAL LINK

Our emotional health also affects our prenatal, pregnancy and postpartum experience. To quote Dr. Rick Hanson in one of his blog posts, "Confronting the Negativity Bias," he explains:

> "The nervous system has been evolving for 600 million years, from ancient jellyfish to modern humans. Our ancestors had to make a critical

decision many times a day: approach a reward or avoid a hazard—pursue a carrot or duck a stick.

Both are important. Imagine being a hominid in Africa a million years ago, living in a small band. To pass on your genes, you've got to find food, have sex, and cooperate with others to help the band's children (particularly yours) to have children of their own: these are big carrots in the Serengeti. Additionally, you've got to hide from predators, steer clear of Alpha males and females looking for trouble, and not let other hunter-gatherer bands kill you: these are significant sticks.

But here's the key difference between carrots and sticks. If you miss out on a carrot today, you'll have a chance at more carrots tomorrow. But if you fail to avoid a stick today— WHAP!—no more carrots forever. Compared to carrots, sticks usually have more urgency and impact. ...

Consequently, your body generally reacts more intensely to negative stimuli than to equally strong positive ones. ...To keep our ancestors alive, Mother Nature evolved a brain that routinely tricked them into making three mistakes: overestimating threats, underestimating opportunities, and underestimating resources (for dealing with threats and fulfilling opportunities). This is a great way to pass on gene copies, but a lousy way to promote quality of life."[1]

Wow! If this explanation doesn't inspire mindfulness of the degree to which your brain is wired to make you afraid, what would it take? Decide to be happy and your wish will be granted. When I was pregnant with Skye, I meditated every single day. I affirmed that my baby was an easy, peaceful, calm baby who laughed a lot and was a joy to be around. When I tell you that Skye has the most delightful, beautiful and funny disposition, I smile knowing my daily meditations and affirmations played a role in manifesting the bright light I call my Skye.

Let's Talk Physical

MAMAHH Moments also affect us on a physical level. We talked about how our thoughts change our genes. Our physical body and the health of that body are of equal importance to our vitality and well-being.

Take a moment to check in with your physical body and ask yourself what is ailing you. Are you feeling 100 percent and if not, what can you do to optimize your health? High-quality, nutrient-dense nutrition is extremely important for your body as well as that bundle of deliciousness you are harvesting right now or in the future.

And, if babe has already joined the world and you are a nursing Mama, you definitely need to upgrade your food choices. And, even still, if you have decided not to nurse for whatever reason, your body is in an intense recovery phase postpartum and will inevitably benefit greatly from proper nourishment.

While reading this book, I hope you are realizing that you are in the driver's seat. Your body is smarter than you and it's ready to take you where you want to go... you just need to learn how to listen to it.

EXPANDING INTO THE SOCIAL DIMENSION

In the beginning, you may feel alone. Perhaps you are the first of your friends or siblings to have children. Or maybe your friends and family are not geographically close to you. Or maybe you just have a difficult time asking for help. Regardless of the what, it's important to build a social network, a tribe, a community. You Are NOT Alone!

> *"Friendship is the only cure for hatred, the only guarantee of peace."*
> —Buddha

As Mamas, we are responsible for a lot. Like the health and well-being of ourselves isn't enough, now we are responsible for raising, molding, and shaping each and every aspect of our offspring. Every response, reaction, and decision we make is being absorbed by our children. They are always watching us, even when we think they are distracted with toys, or iPods, or whatever. They are listening. They are seeing how we communicate with our spouses or partners, our friends, our extended family, and ourselves.

They are like little sponges soaking up everything! From the time they are born until they are seven years old, it's as if their mind is a camera, recording and downloading everything they see, feel, and hear. It's all going into their minds and making an imprint into their bodies. Dr. Maria Montessori, creator of Montessori education, sums up this phenomenon in the term "The Absorbent Mind," which she calls "a marvelous gift to humanity."[2]

When you stop to think about the enormity of a Mama's responsibility, it can be quite overwhelming, this idea that our kids are absorbing absolutely everything. When your children are going through transitions (e.g., teething, growth spurts, adjusting to school, etc.) and they are "misbehaving" or downright driving you bonkers, it is easy to feel like you are going to lose your mind.

And, guess what? That is OK. Feeling overwhelmed and angry, resentful and annoyed are all rational feelings. You are allowed to feel that way. It's what you do with those feelings that shapes who you are and, in turn, how your children will view you and the world around them. And please don't turn to social media for validation because you'll rarely find it there. For a long time, I was anti-Facebook, for several reasons. But, these are the two main ones:

1) If I wasn't talking to you on a regular basis, there was probably a reason.
2) Generally speaking, it appeared to me that the only things people posted were pictures and posts about how *happy, amazing, and perfect* their lives are.

I call bullshit. It's so easy to post all the great moments, the pictures where you look stunning and where your family is smiling and happy. I've yet to see pictures of the behind-the-scenes moments when you are frustrated, angry, annoyed, and overall feeling like running down the street screaming like a banshee. (Maybe I'm the only one that feels like doing that, LOL.)

Granted, I completely understand why it is common practice to post the flowers-and-sunshine moments in our lives. But when you are feeling down in the dumps and want to commiserate with a fellow Mama, scrolling through Facebook may not be the most therapeutic option. Unless, you are a part of our Facebook Tribe @PeacefulMamas where you will always receive honesty, love and support!

Pride can certainly get in the way. Thinking we can (and therefore should) or have to do everything by ourselves can certainly creep into our minds. Being everything to everyone all the time. Wanting to be Super Mama, taking care of your home, your children, yourself… whether you are a stay-at-home Mama or a working Mama, the feelings are the same.

It's normal—wanting to feel like you are doing the best possible job. Looking at yourself in the mirror at the end of the day and being proud of all the decisions that you have made. Knowing that you are presenting the best version of yourself so that your children are witnessing behavior you would want and "expect" of them.

So, what am I getting at? Being in the Mama trenches ain't a piece of gluten-free vegan cake! It is very easy to

For more support, accountability, connection, and motivation on your Peaceful Mama path, consider joining the Peaceful Mama Virtual Circle. It will give you an opportunity to connect with us and our published experts, and to join an online community of conscious mamas.

Learn more at
PeacefulMamas.com/peacefulmamacircle

feel like you are alone, like you are the sole provider for the mind, body, and spirit of these little humans. Which is why creating community is essential. Having a support system where you can feel totally comfortable and confident is mandatory. We need to feel safe and supported and encouraged and be reminded that we are human. It is absolutely vital to our sanity. There's no coincidence that the words community, communal, and communication all have the same prefix. According to dictionary.com: com means: "with," "together," "in association," and (with intensive force) "completely."

So, when we are a part of a community, we feel loved and supported. We feel complete and at peace knowing that we share in the responsibility of child rearing. To me, it feels like a weight lifted off a Mama's shoulders. We have all heard the adage "it takes a village to raise a child." This could not possibly be more accurate. Back in the day, it was common for families to live in the same house with multiple generations so everyone could help raise the children.

Nowadays…not so much.

Consider this golden nugget from H. Jackson Brown, author of *Life's Little Instruction Book:* 90 percent of your happiness is related to your partner in life. That's 90 percent!!! And he doesn't mean that it's up to your partner who will make you happy 90 percent of the time—it's 100 percent up to you to make life-affirming choices regarding the company you keep. So make sure that you are surrounding yourself with people that bring out the best in you.

When you are feeling overwhelmed, please remember this—you are not alone. You are a warrior. You are capable and able. Begin surrounding yourself with Mamas who have values similar to your own. Who are able to lift you up when you are submerged in the sleep-deprived chaos. Cultivate the relationships and friendships in your life that fill up your bucket. You will all reap the benefits for years to come.

EMBRACING THE SPIRITUAL ASPECT

"An Alchemist is someone who transforms everything with Love.
Be an Alchemist. Better yet, just be Love."

—Dashama Konah

For a long time, I didn't know what I believed in. I resonate with Judaism because I was born Jewish and was brought up with that as my heritage and culture. However, I didn't really know what I, in my own mind and heart, thought about spirituality. I began to practice self-discovery and found that it is one of life's most cherished gifts we can give ourselves. Learning to not only love yourself but contriving the meaning behind your existence will bring you to a place of peace and true contentment. This journey reveals that we have the innate ability to tap into our inner being and develop our future success and usefulness.

Our energetic field of power has the ability to attract anything we desire into our lives. The possibilities and potential prospects are infinite. In order to use our intrinsic ability to discover our purpose, we need to become aware of the mind chatter in our heads. Our thoughts are energy, our physical bodies are energy, our relationships are energy—we are filled and surrounded with energy from the universe and its electric field.

When we use these energetic thoughts in a beneficial way, we are contributing to the betterment of the world. And, when we give to the world, we feed our souls purpose. It is a circle. A circle of being, a circle of energy. A ripple effect, where one thought or action will influence or impact the next thought or action. What we often don't realize is that we have countless opportunities every day to positively feed ourselves, which will then feed others. Approach *everything* with love.

The spiritual teacher Byron Katie is a world-renowned author and healer who believes there is only one thing that creates stress or other negative emotions in our lives: our thoughts and beliefs about what's happening in the moment. Her work is known as "The Work"—and if you look her up, you'll find out why and how The Work leads to this profound spiritual realization. In her words, "I discovered that when I believed my thoughts, I suffered, but that when I didn't believe them, I didn't suffer, and that this is true for every human being. Freedom is as simple as that. I found that suffering is optional. I found a joy within me that has never disappeared, not for a single moment. That joy is in everyone, always."

The Work is one of those go-to resources that inspires me to look at my relationship with myself. For instance, it reminds me to check in: can I sit with my hand on my heart and just listen to my breath connecting to my heartbeat for two minutes a day? Am I able to sit and enjoy a cup of tea in silence and just hang out with myself?

This simplicity is proof that we don't have to be religious to have spiritual belief in our connectedness to something greater than ourselves. You just have to have faith and trust that there is more to this life than meets the eye. One of the best ways to become connected and find that sense of faith is by practicing the MAMAHH Moments—taking time to put yourself first!

LINDSAY

I remember diving into books, websites, any research I could find the moment I found out I was pregnant. I wanted to learn everything I could about how my body would be changing, what I should be doing, and how the baby would grow inside me in the most optimally healthy way. I wanted to be better so I could give my best to my baby.

There was a lot of information about nutrition, what I should or shouldn't be eating or drinking. I read a lot about movement and ways in which I should and shouldn't be moving my body. But I don't remember reading or being told too much about what I should be doing to keep my emotional and mental state healthy and how that affects my baby. By my third pregnancy, I didn't have as much time to read and I let up on many of the strict requirements I abided by with my first. The general advice now was everything in moderation. I learned to trust myself a little more and do what felt right for me. What a difference!

I don't know if it's because we were in a different place by the time I had my third, around people who are more focused on holistic thinking and living, but I just remember thinking about my overall emotional, mental, and spiritual health and well-being much more than I did with my first pregnancy. By my second pregnancy, we had moved to a house in a wonderful, family-orientated community surrounded by like-minded neighbors and friends where we all felt the importance of eating well and just living more healthfully.

It's interesting to see how big of an impact the people you surround yourself with make on you.

Another factor was age itself. As we get older, we become exposed to more, we read more, and I had learned more about stress and the potentially detrimental effects of too much stress. When we are under stress, we are not our best. When I was just a few years younger, I felt I was less in control of my own thoughts. I was still consumed in feelings of comparison and worry, of trying to prove myself to others instead of realizing that no matter what I do, I can't control what others think of me. I can only control what I think of me. These are things that I still struggle with today, but it has gotten better as I've gotten a little older and learned to bring kind awareness to those thoughts and make a change.

When I was in my first pregnancy at the age of twenty-nine, I was not really in the best place in life. I was working full time at a job that made me happy but I really wasn't feeling fulfilled. I believe when you aren't spending time doing what really lights you up or using your gifts, you lose yourself a bit. I'm not saying to go quit your job. But, having a little side gig or hobby that brings you joy outside of your everyday job can really help your overall well-being. I didn't really have this at the time. I don't think I knew what really brought me joy. I had great friends at work but I always felt like there was some part of me hidden away while I was there. I couldn't make a great contribution if I wasn't using my unique gifts.

I spent most of my days at this job, knowing on some level that it wasn't the right fit for me but not really seeing a way out. It was a great place, I felt comfortable, and I had a lot of flexibility and autonomy that I knew I would need once I had a child and would have to return to work.

The thought of returning to work after having the baby completely haunted me during this time. I knew that I wanted to stay home but that we needed the income. We were in a condo at the time and also knew we would want to buy a home sometime in the near future and we needed to save more. It wasn't an option at this time.

So both of these situations were weighing in on my stress and emotional state. Also, this was a trying time for my husband and me. Bringing a child into the world brings a lot of excitement but there are a lot of things to think about too. We had to get our home ready and I wanted things done sooner and in a different way at times. You would think it would be trying once we had the children, but for us it began during my pregnancy. Maybe our nerves were up and we were anticipating all the changes to come. I just remember having a lot of disagreements at this time. A marriage is hard work, and having kids only compounds that challenge.

This unease undoubtedly played a role in my overall state of wellness during my first pregnancy without my even being consciously aware of it. It's interesting to see how critical awareness is. Awareness is certainly the first step toward living with more consciousness and positive well-being. It's hard for us to recognize even though our body tells us. It's easier to recognize the physical body stuff—the inside emotional stress is easier to push down and avoid, which is doing much greater damage and disabling us from being more aware and present.

Another element I was missing in my first pregnancy was physical movement. I mentioned that I was at an office working all day. I tried to get outside for a walk at lunch and move around as much as I could, but I was mostly stationary during the day. I would go for walks and do yoga once a week, which was a good lift but I wasn't getting as much daily exercise as I used to before pregnancy when I ran regularly. This lack of movement surely affected my emotional state.

At the time of my first pregnancy, I didn't have a big network and community of moms with whom I was friends. I realize now that a lot of what I was going through, other moms feel too. I felt alone in what I was feeling. There are so many new-mom worries we all face. Not talking about these things with other moms made things worse during my first two pregnancies.

I worked at a small company at the time and they didn't offer a maternity-leave policy. So, we would have only one income during the time that I was home. This was stressful too. I am grateful that my husband and I could afford for me to still take three months unpaid but this was a stress as well. It's surprising that the United States is the only developed nation without mandated paid maternity leave. All of these things weigh on us as new parents and this stress affects our growing babies inside us more than I knew at the time. When there is unease in any aspect of our life, we feel it across all the areas. Even if it's not evident all the time, it's there, heavy and burdensome.

I read many of the recommended pregnancy books, but I didn't really know what to expect when it came to all the things happening to me emotionally and how to deal with them. Too often we feel like we're alone in some of the negative things we think about when we are expecting. We think it should be this rosy happy time, but there are a lot of things we are going through with ourselves and our relationships. Having more tools to get through this time would have been so helpful to me.

When my son, Calvin, came into the world, I was so happy and relieved that he was here. I was anxious and excited to be a mom and to be home with him during maternity leave. But as I talked about earlier, his birth was so much different than I ever envisioned. Recovering from the C-section was so hard. It was really traumatic, so as I look back I have to wonder how all these things weighed in and how they affected Cal.

Cal's first few months were so difficult. He was not the baby who was calm and cried only when he was upset. He cried a lot. There was nothing we could do for hours upon hours as he would cry and nothing would console him. I just thought this is how it was with a newborn. I just went with it. We were giving our whole selves to caring for the baby and very little for ourselves and our relationship together. Remembering to take care of each other was essential but hard to prioritize.

I still loved being home with Calvin, even as he cried most of the day. I know not everyone feels this way, not everyone has the temperament to stay home, but it just works for me. This is not to say it wasn't hard. I was enlivened by the good moments enough that I could feel I was more passionate about this than I ever felt at work.

I would just walk with him in those first few months. He was calm when we moved. The hours of walking everyday helped me and him. And after a few months, his mood did improve dramatically. He was classic "colic," as they described in the books with very little information about it. I applied the various techniques offered but they didn't work for him. Though the more I read, the less I really understood what "colic" was.

However, fascinating new research is coming out from James McKenna, director of the Mother-Baby Behavioral Sleep Lab, and his team of researchers at Notre Dame. They are finding that colic is rooted in the baby's developing respiratory control system. The team also proposed that what causes an infant's vulnerability to colic may be the same as what makes an infant at risk for sudden infant death syndrome (SIDS).

"The origin of both colic and SIDS may be related to the gradual emergence of an infant's ability to voluntarily control the release of air through the vocal tract, learned skills that are required for the development of speech. McKenna points out that infants are susceptible both to colic and SIDS during the same narrow developmental window, between about six to 14 weeks—the time period during which the respiratory system is learning how to shift between voluntary and involuntary control of breathing that involves both the "thinking" part of the brain (the cortex) and the brain stem."[3]

This model is still a theory but testing is underway, and it's certainly an interesting development that will hopefully promote more research into both SIDS and colic, where there is still so little known. I don't know for sure why my firstborn was so much more challenging than my second two but I have since learned how impactful the emotional state of a mother is on her child, even beginning in utero. And, this evidence has been proven for decades. Today, both animal and human studies support that maternal stress and anxiety during pregnancy can have effects on offspring.

The experiences of pregnancy and birth shape mother and child forever. It's not just the feelings a mother has about her own pregnancy; she could be feeling things from her own birth and experience as an infant and child. There is growing research on the lasting impressions that stick with us from those early experiences—the positive and negative.

"We feel there is healing that can happen before conception and during pregnancy to improve a child's chances of healthy emotional development before and after birth, and that is where MAMAHH Moments come in."

~ Lindsay & Natalie

The beautiful thing is that becoming a mother is a way to grow through some of the beliefs we hold inside that no longer serve us. We are able to reflect on these feelings that come up through experiences with our babies. The experiences with our children bring out the parts in us that need to heal and grow. As we learn to be more aware, accepting, and forgiving, emotional healing begins and spiritual breakthroughs can happen. Our children are here to teach us and it's never too late to begin learning.

So our own early experiences factor in, along with our current state and what's going on with us emotionally, mentally, and physically as we are growing a baby inside us. We feel there is healing that can happen before conception and during pregnancy to improve a child's chances of healthy emotional development before and after birth, and that is where MAMAHH Moments come in. There *are* tools that can help us during this critical time. It's not something that will come up at regular prenatal visits with our doctors. It makes sense because the doctors are just looking at the physical—not the mental, emotional, and spiritual. But we're learning how important our mental health is—current research suggests it's just as essential as the physical—so we should start giving it just as much emphasis during pregnancy and beyond.

Dr. Elysia Davis and other researchers at the University of Denver, for example, have spent years studying the effect a pregnant woman's stress reactions have on their babies. Davis and her team have focused their study on the hormone cortisol, which is produced in our body as a reaction to stress and passes through the placenta to the unborn child.

We need the hormone cortisol during pregnancy. We can expect our cortisol levels to naturally increase by two to four times during pregnancy. But when they studied expecting mothers with cortisol levels consistently higher than normal early in the pregnancy and their newborns, they found that these infants displayed a much higher sensitivity to stress and anxiousness than other babies into toddlerhood.[4] After reading about this study, I couldn't help but think about my own pregnancies and how my own stress levels affected my babies.

Stress can increase for a number of reasons and several studies have shown that problems such as daily hassles, pregnancy-specific anxiety, and relationship strain can all have adverse effects on the developing baby during pregnancy. This was very interesting to me because I don't know a single Mama who completely lacks stress, so why aren't we given more tools for coping with stress?

It seems like there should be more public health education about this issue, and pregnant women should be encouraged to look after themselves emotionally and to be able to get help if needed. I wish I had been. Most anxiety and depression in pregnant women is undetected and untreated—and if that's not enough, we are learning how much this negatively affects our children, so why aren't we doing more about it?

The silence about these issues is reflective of our culture as a whole on mental illness. It's something that's not talked about for the most part. Depression is one of the greatest issues affecting moms yet it's brushed under the rug too much because moms are supposed to be happy.

As someone who has the temperament for little children and truly feels most passionate and alive when I am with them, I can attest that it's not all joy with a new baby. There are immensely tough times too. I think I was lucky that I lived near family and was able to get help. My husband was supportive and relieved me when he got home. We made it through those first months together and it made our relationship stronger—though it did strain it in immeasurable ways. Not all of us get those opportunities to recharge and that is what we need. We all need a tribe and tools in our belt to support us during this time.

I've read that depression can be defined as believing we are the only ones who don't deserve compassion. We are giving so much of ourselves to our babies, especially in the early months, when we aren't getting much back. We aren't given any time for ourselves and we are so hard on ourselves. Every moment is basically for our children and we believe that is all there is. We can lose ourselves, our spousal relationship, and our social life if we haven't built our tribe. And we can feel so alone, like we are the only mom who can't pull ourselves together.

By the time I had Lucy, I was in a really different place emotionally, physically, and mentally—and I started practicing MAMAHH Moments. I didn't call it that at the time, but when I was practicing the components of MAMAHH Moments throughout the day, my days were better. I could better handle the ups and downs of pregnancy and being a Mama and all the stresses that come with that.

My state of being was so different when I was pregnant with Lucy than with Calvin. We moved into a house. We made friends with other families who had similar-aged kids. I was still working but we decided that I would stay home with Lucy and Cal after maternity leave. I would find out if my company would be open to me working part-time after maternity leave and if they weren't, I would not return and would stay home full-time. This immensely improved my emotional state, knowing I would be home with them.

I liked the idea of working part-time so I hoped my company would be open to it, but when the time came, they said that it wouldn't work. I was a little sad at first but eventually saw it as the blessing it was. I loved being home. I knew I would need to build a network of other stay-at-home moms to really make it work and I did that. I built my tribe and that made all the difference. I didn't want to feel isolated and knew how important it was not to be, so I just put myself out there. That was the abundance. I made sure I was filling my world with the people and experiences I needed to raise me up not bring me down. I was living in total abundance.

Our life really got into sync by this time. Having a toddler at home meant we already established a great routine. We were eating healthy dinners, most nights. We stayed really active by simply keeping up with him and doing things on the weekend as a family. Going on walks. Also Dan and I found our groove. There wasn't as much uncertainty as when I got pregnant the first time. He had established himself more in his career and as a couple we were communicating and functioning with ease. That contributed to the health and movement pieces.

A lot of positive things were happening in our life when Lucy Mae came to the world in the Fall of 2013. It's funny because at the time of having Calvin, I thought I was OK. But that was just it. I was OK, I wasn't totally happy because while everything looked just right on the outside, I was missing something inside. We are meant to be feeling joyful. Yet, so many of us settle for less than because we are preoccupied with things that we think will make us happy, things that come from our culture, our upbringing, our "keeping up with the Joneses." Once we connect with our inner self, which comes out of practicing MAMAHH, we realize that joy only comes from within, not from things. Everything changes when we start living from our own true heart because we begin attracting everything we truly desire.

Luckily, becoming a parent is the best way to ground you to the salt of the earth, to help you embrace a more heartfelt, authentic way of living. Because children are light and love. Their joyful essence inspires us to live better. We want to give them the love they give us. Having Calvin sparked so many positive changes in my life. Now, I am able to put things into perspective and let go of the unimportant things more easily. While I was still in a career that wasn't totally for me, I saw something else on the horizon. I had a vision of something different and knew every day I was closer to achieving it.

Everything felt good as we went to the hospital to meet our new baby. We had a planned C-section, which took out so much of the uncertainty and stress that we experienced at Calvin's birth. We knew more of what to expect. So while responsibilities rise and free time nearly diminishes when the second child arrives, the stress lowers because you are trusting yourself more and know you can do it.

Lucy came into the world calm and stayed that way as a baby. The first couple months were very tough as we navigated a toddler and a baby and figured out our new routines and roles and got used to less sleep overall. But she could be consoled by nursing or being held. Things that never worked for Calvin, completely calmed Lucy and she was truly content most of the time—which enabled me to stay calm too. Or was it vice versa? Was I actually calmer, which made her calm too? It's hard to know for sure, but going back to the research studies, not only does my state during pregnancy affect her, so does my state as a new mom. When I can stay calm and confident and choose love over fear and do all the things to lessen stress and center myself, the baby responds. Our children are a mirror into our inner selves.

When I got pregnant with Paige when Lucy was just eight months old, I was really in a good place. I felt like I was exactly where I should be. The days were long, but I loved being home with Cal and Lucy. There was so much to explore and we did it a lot together. I was ready for more children even though mine were still young; I couldn't wait to bring another child into the world. I got a lot of negative reactions from people when I started to share my news. They asked, was it an accident? Are you sure you can handle this? But it forced me more than ever to trust myself. I felt good about this decision and other people are going to think whatever they want and I cannot control that.

"When moms are better, children are better. When our children are better, our world becomes a place with more kindness, love, and compassion. It's not about creating a better world for our children but creating better children for our world."

~ Lindsay

I didn't have that same confidence when I was pregnant with Calvin. I'm sure it came from being in a better place, from finding my groove, from really feeling like I was living in a way that was and is aligned with my true purpose. Mindfulness became a regular practice for me around this time. I made time for quiet stillness every morning. And I was learning about ways that I could re-center myself when negative vibes crept up on me throughout the day. A negative experience didn't deplete me as it once did. A shift in me was taking place as I started trusting myself and following my heart. I remained committed to the process because I could see how positively this vibrational flow was affecting me and everyone around me, especially my children.

When I think about my emotional state at this time, it was mostly positive. I was with my children all day, and they were sleeping all night, so my husband and I had time together in the evenings—we had time for ourselves and each other. In my free time, I actually started writing a blog about parenting and motherhood. People wondered how I stayed so calm, how I made time for anything, how I stayed happy. I felt encouraged to write about my motherhood experiences because I felt most alive and enlivened when I did it. I was connecting the two things I loved most—motherhood and writing—and it was filling me up. Writing became an act of affirmation. I wrote about the challenges, how I was growing through it, and the things I loved about motherhood and this helped me connect with my inner voice and begin paying more attention to the words I was using and how I was communicating. I was practicing affirmations and experiencing positive results from it without really even realizing I was doing it. It is so powerful.

It's amazing how you can attract the things you want in life by just thinking differently. Around this time, my former company reached back out to me to help them out with a project and they were going to let me do it on my own terms. I could work from home, set my own hours, and pick up more as I wanted. It felt perfect. I was able to line up some childcare and I was doing the thing I always hoped—staying home and doing some work part time remotely. The social part of me was getting filled up too because I went into the office occasionally and connected with colleagues and friends. We had some extra money again so Dan and I could go out to dinner and go on date nights.

And by chasing around two children, I was keeping in great shape. We were eating well for the most part. Movement and Health were keys to this overall positive shift. Life was good and continued that way throughout my pregnancy. I was in a really good place mentally, emotionally, and physically. Such a different place than when I was pregnant with Calvin, when there was so much uncertainty and a lack of confidence in myself. I was still writing my blog and I even started doing some personal development work up until Paige was born in February of 2015. I thought we couldn't have had a calmer baby than Lucy but Paige was a delight. She was the sweetest, most patient and calmest little baby. She adored watching her older siblings. She slept longer and faster than the first two and she fed well. We called her our little Zen Baby.

Eventually I started feeling the pull of all the different things going on in my life from working and I wasn't able to keep up my blog. I really started to feel like I wasn't juggling it all well anymore. It's always a juggle but it's about finding the juggle that works for you. I began to feel like it wasn't working for me anymore. I wasn't filling my own bucket. Realistically, every area in our life won't be fully balanced, but we must find the juggle that's right for us. It comes from listening within, trusting, and taking steps toward the areas where we need healing or more attention. It's always evolving as we grow. We have to be aware and open to making changes until we find our own unique balance that feels right.

As I look back on my three pregnancies over the past five years, it paints a pretty clear picture of how strongly my own emotional, mental, and physical state affects me and my babies. It seems so clear as I look back. At the time, it didn't seem so clear. That is why we need to proactively follow MAMAHH Moments and be versed in these tools so we can better recognize when we are losing awareness and centeredness and can make shifts to get to a more positive state.

Some of us have so much noise in our minds and our lives that we aren't even conscious of another way of living. We may be so deep into a negative state that we don't even see glimpses out of it. We know hormones of pregnancy and all the stresses of pregnancy and being a new mom can bring us into this state. We need to support one another in being more aware and sharing the tools to be better—more well, mindful, connected and purposeful—so we don't get on the negative track and feel there is no way out.

When moms are better, children are better. When our children are better, our world becomes a place with more kindness, love, and compassion. It's not about creating a better world for our children but creating better children for our world. Within all of us is kindness, love, and wisdom—and when we feel this love within, then we can give back that immense love and compassion to our children.

CHAPTER 4

GETTING REAL

Not Losing Ourselves in the Juggle of Being Me, a Wife, and a Mama

NATALIE

Let's get real for a moment, shall we? Yes—Mamahood is a glorious and miraculous blessing. With that said, it is also important to note that your patience will be tested, you will have days/weeks/months and sometimes even years where you may feel like you are never going to get a restful night's sleep. In the early weeks and months, you may walk around like a zombie trying to decipher if it's a Monday or a Friday. Your main concern seems to be how many wet diapers you have seen that day and if you brushed your teeth. Snuggling up to your spouse and watching a funny movie may seem like a thing of the past. You might feel like you traded in your individuality and personality for car seats and a Mama mobile.

And, it might seem like you will never have a routine again. Just know, nearly everything you are feeling and experiencing is completely normal.

Why do I say "nearly everything"? Because there are circumstances where professional help is required. And, in the haze of those early days, you may not have the resources to diagnose if what you are experiencing requires outside help. *It's important that prior to giving birth, you have a list of friends and practitioners you can call upon at any hour in the event that you do need extra help.* You might even start by checking out our list of Peaceful Mama Experts at PeacefulMamas.com to help you envision the types of healers and practitioners that belong on your Individual Support System List.

A Tribe is a Must for a Mama

When I was a first time Mama, my Angel of Light, Jonah, cried nonstop. When one of my best friends asked me how everything was going for us, I told her that every time he nursed it felt like shards of glass were on fire in my breasts. I explained that my nipples were raw and blistered and I clenched every muscle in my body in pure agony as he nursed, eight to ten times a day. But, I was determined to nurse for a year. And, looking back, I'm not sure what my game plan was exactly. I suppose with my priorities and goals set high, I probably would have continued suffering had I not talked to Marisa about that.

She told me I needed a lactation consultant—fast. I am SO grateful I took her advice and found someone to come help me. Even though I was aware that many Mamas hire lactation consultants, at first I was concerned about the cost, the effectiveness, and if I "really" needed someone to help me with breastfeeding. I mean, I'm a woman. Shouldn't it just be natural? The whole reason women have breasts is so that they can feed their babies. So, did I need an outsider to teach me how to do that? And, did I need another feel-like-a-failure moment?

Feeling like a failure when your hormones are trying to regulate, when you are sleep deprived, when you are in pain, and when your entire life has just completely changed can be a recipe for disaster. Which is one of the reasons why we recommend creating a list of potential practitioners, healers, friends, doctors, and family members that can help if necessary—the network of people in your Individual Support System should be people you trust and they should be people who jive with your personal belief system, morals, and values.

I cannot emphasize enough how important this is to do before your bundle of deliciousness arrives. Pre-planning will save you time, brain-power, and emotional heartache in the future, guaranteed. Or if you don't have time for this, consider hiring a postpartum doula. Their role is to provide practical, informational, and emotional support to families. They come with that trusted list of resources as well as a wealth of other support and nurturing care during that delicate time with your newborn. And, if you were unable to get a copy of this book while pregnant and are reading it as a new Mama, then hats off to you for taking the time to read this book now!!! Either way, we are honored and humbled that you have stumbled upon our book.

Back to lactation, and how it led me to create my support system. In my desperation, I pushed my ego aside and made an appointment with a local lactation consultant. The best part was that she could come to my house! And thank you divine grace and universe and everything holy and sacred for that because not only did Jonah cry at home, his cry intensified tenfold when we put him in his car seat. So, the fact that I didn't have to traumatize either one of us further by getting in the car was monumental.

The lactation consultant was wonderful. She helped guide me with different positions, opening his mouth a little wider for an easier latch, etc. She also gave me one of the best recommendations I have ever received, which was the name of International Board Certified Lactation Consultant, Jennifer Tow.

The reason she referred me to Jennifer was because I suspected that my acid reflux issues could potentially be contributing to Jonah's discomfort. Jennifer Tow was well known for her Holistic Mothering and Lactation groups, so I quickly made a Skype appointment with her.

JT, as we call her, is one of the most knowledgeable and passionate women I know. She changed the course of my life and motherhood. If you are having breast-feeding issues, or your baby or child is suffering and you don't know who to turn to, she would be my first recommendation.[5] Her passion is fierce, her wisdom is decades ahead of our time, and the proof is in the pudding, as they say, because after following her advice, participating in her webinars, and connecting with other Mamas she has helped, my education skyrocketed and my life forever changed—in a nutshell, I would not be where I am now without my support system!

Unfortunately, I do not think enough Mamas are talking about the trials and tribulations. The tough times and the shameful times. Mama guilt is legit. There are some days I ask myself if I am qualified to even be a mother. And, of course there are other days I am filled with pride for the choices I have made. Yet this chapter focuses a little more on how the challenging moments of Mamahood help us grow individually and if played properly, help our relationships grow too.

Whoever said we are supposed to be perfect? Nobody, but too often we try to live up to that false ideal. Unfortunately, doing so leaves us feeling defeated or like asking for help makes us "less than." We love Jessica Alba and all she stands for. This is a truth we need to hear more of:

"Being perfect is being flawed, accepting it,
and never letting it make you feel less than your best."

—Jessica Alba

I'm very blessed to have lifelong girlfriends (a.k.a. my "Rotag Sistas") who are going through Mamahood around the same time as me. We have a support system and can call on each other whenever necessary. And, although I really wish we all lived closer, I am super grateful that we have phones and we can be completely vulnerable with each other.

Sometimes we even get lucky and one of them will come for a visit. When one of my best friends, Heidi, vacationed in our home, we juggled four kids between us and somehow were still able to catch up on each other's lives, laugh, cry, commiserate, and support each other.

Having a support group or tribe, especially during Mamahood, is probably the most important factor in maintaining peace in your life. Remember, that when I say peace I am referring to balance, calmness, joy, and love and some days—it might simply mean regaining your sanity.

Five Tools of the Tribe

One of the things we spoke about at length was how challenging young children are and how much they need us to provide them with tools to deal with life and whatever comes along. It is so easy for us to say "do this" and "do that" and "we expect you to behave like this and that." But if we are not being role models of that type of behavior, how are we to expect them to do as we say?

I constantly have to remind myself that being a Mama is a lifelong journey and process. And, that the more effort I put into bettering myself as a parent, a communicator, and a wife, the bigger the rewards for everyone. It is important to have clear and specific intentions to model for my kids.

Let me preface this by saying, I am by *no stretch* of the imagination an expert in raising children. There are things that I say, do, and think that would not award me with Mama of the Year.

Like what, you ask? Oh, you know—shouting at the top of my lungs, roaring like a lion, walking out of the room in an attempt to gain back my sanity, etc.

With that being said, any tricks that I find helpful it's my pleasure to share them with you.

Here are five tools that I have found to be very helpful. I hope you find them useful as well!

1. Get Down to Their Level and Make Eye Contact

Meet them at eye level. Whenever I stop what I'm doing (cooking, cleaning, texting, etc.) and get down to my kids' level, the energy automatically shifts. They feel important and special and realize that I am listening to them. We often talk about "respect" and as much as I want my children to respect me, it is equally important that I show them respect as well. Meeting them eye to eye is a powerful way to embody it.

2. Turn It Into a Game or Imaginative Play

Somewhere along the way we forgot how much fun it is to play. Children are hardwired to learn by playing. Let yourself get creative, and almost anything can be turned into a game or storytelling. For example, there are times when we have to leave the house and I notice that my eagerness to get in the car is usually resisted. But, when I say, "Who is gonna get in the car the quickest?" suddenly getting out of the house is a breeze! Or, when getting their clothes on becomes putting on all the pieces of their lion costume. The more clothes they get on the louder the roar. Tap into your imagination and you're speaking their language. Set an intention to keep this in the back of your head: "How can we make this fun?"

3. Sing It

I don't know about your kids, but my boys looooove music. So, if hubs and I break out into song to encourage brushing teeth, life gets easier. Plusssss, it's pretty fun making up silly songs with your kids. Children just respond to our voices better when it is in song. They don't care if you can carry a tune or stay on beat. Just sing it and they listen and enjoy it more.

4. Have Them Repeat the Expectation

Sometimes I feel like I'm talking to a wall, like nobody is listening and I'm just rambling with a sleeping audience. It's aggravating and exhausting. Who wants to feel like a nag?

Raise your hand, please.

Oh. No one? Yeah, that's what I thought. I find that asking children to repeat the expectations makes it much easier on everybody. Communication is key. For example, before we go to a playdate or a birthday party, we will have a chat in the car on the way there. It will go a lil' somethin' like this: "Jonah, we are going to Yoni's house. I trust you to make kind and loving choices and to be a good listener. When I call your name, no matter what you are doing, I know you will walk over to me and say, 'Yes, mama.' Please make this fun and easy for us. Won't it feel good to be proud of yourself when we get back in the car?"

"Yes, mama." OK, so what did I say? And, then he will usually sum it up in his own words. Or the other option is, "What did you say again, Mama?" At which point, I try to take my own advice and Choose to Chill before responding with "That hurts my feelings that you didn't listen to me the first time." Hey, you can't win them all—LOL.

5. Make Sure They Participate in the Solution

When resolving a problem that affects you, your child, and maybe even the whole family, make sure they have helped come up with the idea—a.k.a. participated in the brainstorming session to find a solution.

It's not easy being a child. Imagine always being told what to do, how to do it, and when—that would pretty much suck. So, one of the ways we can have compassion and increase the likelihood of follow-through and excitement about a solution is by having our children contribute their ideas in problem solving. When Jonah helps me come up with a solution, he is an active participant in the process and is excited to help. For example, he wasn't feeling 100 percent the other day and wanted to eat crackers.

I told him we wanted him to eat really clean until he felt better.

This quickly led to a meltdown.

So we wrote down on a piece of paper: "When Jonah feels 100%, he can eat crackers."

And, then I asked him what else he wanted to do and eat when he was feeling better and he gave me additional ideas, which I added to the list.

Hello, game changer!

He was very pleased to have participated in the list, which we posted on the fridge.

Of course, rationalizing with an infant is not always possible. The plus side to that is they are not capable of saying things that make your blood boil. But, some of the same rules apply to your youngest ones, for example: looking them in the eye, turning things into games, repeating yourself, singing and being consistent with your baby.

Basically, kids want to feel important too…as they should!

Mastering Communication 101 for Mamas

Remember that being a parent is not just about raising children. It is also about raising the bar for yourself. Personal growth and development is one of the keys to successful and meaningful relationships in your family. If your goal is to create a beautiful, lifelong bond between you and your children and a family legacy, then that is going to take dedication, commitment, and work. It also means meeting your dark side and forgiving yourself (and your spouse and your children) for their faults.

"The quality of life is the quality of your relationships."

—Anthony Robbins

Remember the outside world—including everything we observe in our relationships—is a reflection of what's going on with us. Our family and friends mirror back to us the work we need to do on ourselves. One of the best ways to begin working on personal growth and development is by fine-tuning the art of communication.

Clear communication is totally crucial.

When I was in college, many moons ago, my intention was to dance. My major was Dance Performance and Education. As time went on, I realized that perhaps dancing should not be my main focus. So, while I continued to dance, I entered a new path where I began taking classes in Mass Communications.

This was where my love for writing and speaking could be cultivated. It was when I began learning about how specific and clear one must be when communicating because everything is open to interpretation. *Everything.*

Improving our communication is a skill that rarely becomes mastered. Instead it is an ongoing practice throughout our lives, one that can inevitably help create the life of your dreams *or* can manifest a less than idyllic reality. Only you have that control. It's called free will.

When we are crystal clear in our thoughts, feelings and desires then the Universe/God/Creator (however you name it) completely understands what it is we desire.

You know those people who just automatically make you feel comfortable? Like the energy around them is inviting and welcoming? These people are communicating love through their actions, reactions, and energetic vibe—a.k.a. verbal and nonverbal communication. Certain people have a propensity to function like this because of their personality and social conditioning. It may come more naturally to some and be slightly more challenging for others. However, it is an evolutionary skill and everyone's could use a little polishing.

Communication is more than talking. Communication is also about actively listening. Creating a safe and welcoming space for the person you are with and being fully present with them. Looking someone in their eyes when they speak to you, especially children. Getting down to their level and showing them with your physical body that you are present and available. Responding with head nods, smiles, or a gentle hand on their arm. These are all ways we can actively listen. Showing love without words.

Additionally, when we are communicating we must accept the love of others as they can give it—because everyone communicates in their own personal way. If you haven't already read the *Five Love Languages* by Gary D. Chapman, I highly recommend it. The author clearly explains how we all respond to and require varying forms of love. It is an excellent resource for the different ways people innately communicate.

Communication is absolutely mandatory in every relationship. When we are doing all the talking, we are very rarely doing much listening. That may seem obvious, but when you really think about having a conversation with people, ask yourself if you are thinking about the next thing that you are going to say versus fully receiving what the other person is saying.

Oftentimes when we are "listening," we are not listening to understand the other person, but instead we are listening to see if we agree or disagree with what they are saying. When we are focusing on agreeing or disagreeing, what we are actually doing is judging or objectifying the other person. It may not be a "negative judgment" per se, but the intention is still the same. And when we are living in judgment of others and ourselves, we are actually missing out on the uniqueness and beauty that emanates from our loved ones.

It's *all about* coming from a place of wonder and curiosity about that person. When someone is sharing something with you, try to tune into what lights that person up and what you can do to nurture and support them. Come from a space of really seeing them and their unique self. We all see, feel, and express things in every moment. You want to be conscious and aware of what your story is versus what their story is—you want to expand your listening ear to make room for both. Just because you would feel or have felt a certain way does not mean that your child, spouse, co-worker, friend feels the same way. You don't want to make assumptions and overlay your story onto them because they may not feel the same way or have interpreted a situation in the same way as you.

Ask yourself and your partner: what are you feeling now? What are you needing now? What is important to you? And what are your values?

Then be ready to receive and understand without bringing your pre-conceived thoughts, opinions, and experiences—be willing to allow for shifts in your perspective.

When we can shift from judgment to understanding, all of the relationships in our lives will positively change. A Peaceful Mama does her best to avoid compartmentalizing friends and family and anyone we come in contact with, from the cashier at the grocery store to our children's teachers. She comes from a place of love and equality for all.

When we embrace people with love and understanding, we are showing them compassion. And, having compassion for others allows you to have compassion for yourself. Practice embodying compassion because we are living our human experience and in doing so we want to honor and respect the soul's journey.

FILLING UP THE FAMILY BUCKET

As a loving wife, mother and friend, I found myself always trying to meet everyone's needs. And, it became quite overwhelming at times, like I was neglecting someone I care for and love deeply.

So, I started asking myself: *how can I, as a conscious Mama, meet everyone's needs while also meeting my own needs?*

In acknowledging my own needs to myself, the magic happened. First and foremost, I remembered in my heart and soul that the most effective way of being the Mama I wanted to be was by choosing myself first. Even though that often means waking up at 4:30 in the morning to fill up my own bucket.

When I wake up before the roosters, I am able to have my alone time. I meditate, read, exercise, catch up on social media, shower, and energetically prepare my home for the day.

If I am unable to do all of the above or any of the above, my day and my mood are significantly different. The choices I make are not well thought out. The responses I have are not my favorite. The reactions I have are less than perfect. So, I actively make an effort every single day to choose me over those extra hours of morning sleep. (Unless of course I have been up all night with a nursing baby.)

Sometimes, the Universe has alternate plans for us—and that's when it's important to just go with the flow. If I'm getting and feeling a lot of resistance around a project or idea I have, then I know it's not the right time for me to place my focus there.

It is so important to not feel drained and taken for granted—let's go with replenished and appreciated! Yet it is so incredibly easy to fall into a pattern of give, give, give without realizing that when you give you are oftentimes taking from your own reserves. The less energy, patience, and connectedness you have for yourself will only cause you to react in a way you may later regret. You don't want to get to a point where you are completely depleted and have diminished your own basic and fundamental priorities.

Remember: you may not ever find balance, but you can *always* choose to find peace in every situation. There can be harmony in your life and in your family. It's a choice—your choice.

On the *Mama Thrive* podcast with Lisa Bogle and Kaya Jongen, they recommend regularly using a technique called a "family sweep." They describe it as an internal mental process. You check in with everyone's energy levels and what your personal connection level is with them at that particular point during the day.

The goal is to identify whose metaphorical bucket needs more love and attention—your Mama intuition will tell you! It is a perfect way to flex your intuition muscle and keep it strong, which cultivates your own confidence and faith in yourself. And, it is extremely important that you also include yourself in this family sweep because quite often you may find that you are the one in need of attention. So, how do you perform a family sweep?

Here are the basics I learned from Lisa and Kaya, with some of my own twists. First, you take a few moments to check in with your own breath and then start to think of each member of your family, one at a time. Mentally check in on them: what's been going on with them today and in the last hour? What do you gauge their emotions as needing and wanting? Are they content, satisfied, and happy—or are they giving off a vibe that leads you to believe their needs are not being met?

How are *you* feeling with them? Are you feeling super connected or disconnected?

As you move onto the next member of the family, you want to use your motherly and wifely intuition as a guide to help you identify who needs the most attention at this particular moment. Are they needing engagement or do they need space? As you visualize this, you may imagine each member of your family as holding a bucket

Natalie's Tale of Self-Care

There are the days when I find myself shouting something like: "I don't care if you have to dance naked standing on your head, I do NOT want to hear crying when I go upstairs!" This eloquent and tweet-able rant was what I shouted to hubs once when I was feeling quite un-Zen and very much in need of some alone time, a.k.a. SELF-CARE!!!

Rewind a few moments earlier to set the scene for ya: I just wanted a few moments to go upstairs, take a shower, and get dressed. Maybe, if time was on my side and my angels were in a good mood, MAYBE I could even shave my legs without having a baby banging on the glass shower door or a young child demanding my immediate attention. Such high hopes I had. Within thirty seconds of my arrival at the top of the stairs, there was crying and whining. That's when I put on my classy gal hat and created that perfectly depicted scenario of dancing on his head naked.

Now, although I was none too pleased when relaying said message to hubby, by the time I got to my room this time around, there was no crying, no shouting, no disarray. I looked at myself in the mirror and busted out laughing. *Where the hell did I come up with that? That was pretty damn funny, if I do say so myself.* OK, deep breaths, get in the shower.

I'm not sure how long it took me to take a shower, get dressed and—yes, I did—shave my legs that day. Both legs. Calves and thighs. I highlight this because there have been plenty of days that I have been in a rush or thinking about twenty other things that I have actually completely forgotten to shave the other leg or done a quick lower leg job. But I remember deliberately thinking: No. Not today. Today, I stand up for myself. Bye, bye, self-sacrifice. I am taking the time I want and deserve to take care of my own needs first. What a concept!

Does it have to be every decision, every day? Do you need to only think about yourself with complete disregard to anyone else? Um, no. That's not what I'm saying. What I'm saying (read SHOUTING) from the Modern Hippie Mama rooftops is this:

"MAMAS, you deserve to take some time to nurture yourself, to nourish yourself, to pamper yourself, to love yourself FIRST!"

Because I can tell you this. That morning I got a little self-care time in, I was a much better version of myself than if I had taken on the day sans shower immediately following the first attempt at "me time."

Some things in life are non-negotiables. For me, self-care is one of them.

Self-care. Totally underrated. Totally necessary.

Please continue to remind yourself that. You Are NOT Alone!

with water in it. How much water do you see in each of their buckets? Your inner sight reveals a direct correlation with how much extra focus they or you may need. And, that's to whom you give your most attention. Dear Mama, not everyone needs all of you all the time!

Learning how to prioritize the needs, desires, and requirements of you and your family can significantly improve your relationships without robbing yourself of much needed attention and love. Scheduling time to fill your and your family's buckets is also super helpful. For example, every Saturday morning my hubs takes the children so I can have a few hours to work, teach , write, etc. He gets alone time with our boys and I am able to fill up my own reserves. Additionally, scheduling in bodywork and energy work is something that our family particularly thrives on. Massage, chiropractic care, acupuncture, etc. Whatever you fancy is great—as long as you actually do it!

Filling your own bucket and then your family's is the essence of self-care.

LINDSAY

Many people refer to the years with young children as the longest shortest years and I couldn't agree more.

The days are long but they are so full of *every* emotion. The highest highs and the lowest lows of my life have happened in the last few years since becoming a mother. Our children challenge every part of us. They really do. But they also bring us to a new level of feeling. We feel love, happiness, gratefulness, joy—and we also feel sadness, loneliness, failure, envy, frustration, and resentment.

Many of us are completely taken aback by all of the negatives we feel after becoming parents. We are surprised, if not shocked, to be feeling these tough emotions about something that is supposed to be positive and beautiful and wonderful.

More information is available now about parenting, the good and the not so good aspects of it. Whenever I am searching something relating to parenting, I keep in mind that our society tends to share our negative experiences more than our positive ones and I do not let others' opinions shade my choices. We must trust our own intuition and not get caught up in worry or judgment. It isn't productive. That may mean limiting our amount of social media and online reading. We should always be asking the question, does what I am doing and reading make me feel up or down? What experience do I want more of? How can I find joy in this? Am I getting a little happier overall?

A powerful tool to help us shift the lens to experience more joy in each moment is appreciative inquiry, developed by David Cooperrider under the guidance of his thesis advisor, Suresh Srivastva. Author Jacqueline Kelm wrote a fascinating, practical book that breaks it down called the *The Joy of Appreciative Living*. It's about how we can create an upward trend in happiness in our lives by following five principles of Appreciative Inquiry. I'll share summaries of Kelm's illuminations at a high level here:

- **The Constructivist Principle:** We are constructing or building our life experience in every moment with our thoughts. This is evident in the experience that multiple people view the same event and each have their own unique account of what happened.
- **The Poetic Principle:** We can find whatever we want in any situation. There is good and bad, beautiful and ugly. It's all there and we find what we pay attention to.
- **The Anticipatory Principle:** Whatever pictures you have in your mind will influence your future. Hello, visualization.
- **The Simultaneity Principle:** Change begins simultaneously in the moment we ask the question. Take the question, "What is one thing I could do today to increase my joy, no matter how small?" By simply asking the question we can focus our thinking and bring happiness to the forefront.
- **The Positive Principle:** Within all of us, every person, situation, or organization, is a positive core that consists of wisdom, knowledge, positive attitudes, and skills to name a few. The more we focus on our innate positive core, the more joy we have. It's a journey and not always easy to see the good, yet the more we work at it the easier it becomes.

We all have a tendency to look for happiness in the big moments when most of our day is made up of little moments. Finding happiness in the little everyday things is how we create big change overtime. I love Jacqueline Kelm's book because she shares a practical framework for achieving greater happiness. Little things we can do moment-to-moment to experience more joy. She also shares about all the latest research in neuroplasticity. At one time, we thought the brain was fixed and stable, but new research is uncovering quite the contrary. We can retrain our mind for greater happiness just as we can train our body for greater fitness.

MAMA, DON'T LET THESE THINGS GET IN THE WAY OF YOUR HAPPINESS

Moms are highly susceptible to negative factors that threaten our happiness. They can all pile up and suddenly we could get into a pessimistic haze where nothing is right, we see no way out, and we feel we don't deserve compassion. The goal should be to bring awareness to these feelings, be kind to ourselves in these moments and do the things that make us feel better, like practicing self-care. Let's go over some of the feelings we may experience so we can proactively help prevent them from taking us over.

Sleep Deprivation. When we are sleep deprived as we are with newborns, it's difficult to see any light. Many moms describe the first few months as a haze. When we aren't getting enough sleep, it is hard to function. I do know that once babies start sleeping longer stretches and Mamas are getting some more sleep, life can resume (somewhat) again and we begin feeling a little more like ourselves. Initially it really is tough. The best thing to do during this time is to build up your village, your tribe. You will need help with your other children, if you have any. So say "yes" to help from anyone who offers. You'll need to take naps whenever you can. You can go to sleep with your children at 7 p.m. and let your husband be with the baby. *Whatever* you can do during these first couple months to get your sleep, try it.

This is not to suggest that exhaustion necessarily takes over—on the contrary. You will find energy you didn't even know you had, and our children rejuvenate us in many ways. Remember that story I shared about early mornings when I was up with a newborn most of the night and had to awake with my other children when they woke up in the morning? Their smiles and presence and joy really did give me some energy that I could not have found on my own.

Somehow the more we have to do, the more we get done. So much of it has to do with our mental state and how we feel about the lack of sleep. When we accept it as par for the course as a new mom, then we can think about other things and not let it take away from our experiences in the present. The body really is amazing and can get by on little sleep when necessary. But, the trick is, my mind had to be OK with this new reality and that was the harder one to convince.

It's no wonder that we are not our best in the early months with a newborn. It's one of the biggest challenges of our life but I believe we can get through it with more calm if we shift our outlook. The more negative we are about it, the more negative our day is, and when we are negative our children feel it and they act up too and have trouble being calm. As the Mama, so much of our energy correlates into the moods of everyone in the house. The MAMAHH Moments help us still make time for self-care and get through this very tough time of parenting with more calm and grace.

Judgment. When we are in a negative state, it's so easy to listen to that voice in our head that is against everyone and everything, including your own self. We all hear it at times. It's up to us to get control of it by accepting what it has to say and then choosing to think something different. The best way to think differently is to take action. The judgmental voice in my head tends to be loudest when I'm not doing anything.

"You only have control over three things in your life—
the thoughts you think, the images you visualize,
and the actions you take."

— Jack Canfield

Our imagination is a powerful tool. We can use it to imagine good outcomes or bad ones. When I'm feeling bad, I challenge myself to examine the thoughts I've created, what I'm envisioning. Is it a productive use of my imagination? Take judgment for example. Judgment is a result of feeling a lack within me and judging another is helping me temporarily feel better about that thing within me that's hurting or I'm avoiding. We can choose a loving thought instead of a fear-based judgment of someone else or of ourselves by someone else. It's up to only us to think, imagine, and act differently. We can use our imagination for the positive or negative.

Brené Brown describes this tendency we all have to judge:

"We judge people in areas where we're vulnerable to shame, especially picking folks who are doing worse than we're doing. If I feel good about my parenting, I have no interest in judging other people's choices. If I feel good about my body, I don't go around making fun of other people's weight or appearance. We're hard on each other because we're using each other as a launching pad out of our own perceived deficiency."

—Brené Brown, Ph.D., LMSW

In essence, when we are feeling good about ourselves and our decisions, we aren't judging. We have no reason to judge. But when we are feeling unhappy with ourselves—in any area of our life—we judge. Why? Because, we think it feels good to perceive that others are doing worse than us or the same as us. Remember, how misery loves company? Well, judgment enjoys a little companionship too. The issue with this is that putting other people down to boost our own ego only pushes us further from our truth. Further from the potential connectedness and possible relationships we could have with our peers. Plus, everything is temporary. We only feel "good" for a short time after we have judged someone else. And, it is only making that ego-negative voice in our head grab the steering wheel when we could all use more heart-led choices instead of ego-driven reactions.

Conclusion? Instead of choosing to judge (consciously or subconsciously) and inevitably feeling worse as a result of that choice, try choosing love. Try choosing compassion. Try choosing to let go of the negative spiral thinking and feeling, and brush yourself with a feather instead of beating yourself with a rock. It is OK to be gentle on yourself. In fact, it is more than OK. It is applauded, recommended, and honored (at least in The Peaceful Mama community, it is.) I've found that parenting is an easy place for us to feel the need to judge because so much of it is unknown and we keep falling short of our ideals. Nobody has it all figured out, and even those who appear to on the outside may be really struggling inside. We don't know. But we do know this: the best thing we can do is to support each other, be honest and open, and just accept our mistakes—because we are all going to make them—and move on to the next thing.

Comparison. The sister of judgment is comparison and neither one is healthy for us but we all find ourselves doing it, especially as we become parents. As we judge others, the next thing we do is compare ourselves to them. And we'll never match up because we are comparing apples to oranges.

It's apples to oranges because parenting is different for every person, just as every child is so unique. Nobody but yourself knows what is right for you and for your children. Yet we spend a lot of time thinking about what we could be doing differently and we base that thinking on what our neighbor or friend or even our own parents did. Some of this is internal and some of it is really coming out from the people who are supposed to love us. Our parents may make comments for how they would do something differently, and the best thing we can do is thank them, take any part of it that is helpful, and then let the rest go. Getting angry about it doesn't help matters—though all of us will do it at times. Our emotions are on high and when we haven't taken time to get to a centered place, we can easily be set off. We don't want to be this way but it's a reality we all face.

This is a great opportunity to go back to "The Work" by Byron Katie. She offers a simple way to challenge these beliefs in our heads, the ones about us not being worthy, or lovable, or wanted, or appreciated. Whatever it is, we can challenge that. She says that another person can say something negative and hurtful to us like "you are not worthy of love" but it only hurts if we believe it. Her powerful work is a meditation. It's about opening our hearts. Ask the questions, then go inside and wait for the deeper answers to surface.

1. Is it true? (The answer is one syllable: yes or no. If no, move to 3.)
2. Can you absolutely know that it's true? (Yes or no.)
3. How do you react, what happens, when you believe that thought?
4. Who would you be without the thought?

Then turn the original thought around. The turnarounds are ways of experiencing the opposite of what you believe. When you have turned the statement around (a statement can often be turned around to the self, to the other, and to the opposite, though sometimes there's just one turnaround), find at least three specific, genuine examples of how the turnaround is true.

This is Byron Katie's process and detailed instructions can be found online at TheWork.com. Her own story is very powerful, and so is The Work—we can't recommend it highly enough.

It goes back to Brené Brown's quote: when we feel good about what we are doing and the choices we are making, we won't be bothered by others' comments or criticisms because *we aren't comparing ourselves to anyone else*. We aren't bothered by it because we trust ourselves and believe we are doing the best we can with the awareness and tools we have now. It doesn't mean we can't share tools for what is working;

we need to do that. It doesn't mean we can't get advice from our parents; it's good to hear about other ideas and methods. We can be open to advice but in the end we have to take or leave it and do what feels right for us. We have to trust that voice within because that is our truth.

We make the best choices when 1) we are being present in the moment, instead of being in a remembering or anticipating mode, 2) when we are being positive and not dwelling in a place of negativity but seeing the good in ourselves and our situation, and 3) when we are being real about what is actually going on and really being us, not the person we see in the book or our neighbor or our mom. We have to be our own unique self and own it.

Discomfort. The discomfort of our body post-labor is not fun. Our body carried a baby and then birthed it into this world. And, that takes time to heal. While that may sound logical as you read this book with your logical mind, postpartum you might try to convince yourself otherwise. Please remember this section. Remind yourself that you are a Warrior and Goddess Princess for everything you are doing and have yet to accomplish. It is a beautiful release to grant yourself permission and grace to accept the delicate, fragile and crucial opportunity for deep healing. Yes, we have the physical discomfort of delivery either vaginally or through cesarean that has to heal. You are correct—it's not exactly what we would call "fun." But the moment we are able to safely start some physical movement or stretching, it does feel good. And, slowly we start to see glimpses of ourselves again. And remember, the internet only magnifies the bad. The horror stories are the exception. Yet, sometimes after a quick surf on the web about anything related to parenting and pregnancy, the worst-case scenario seems to be the norm. Don't let others' experiences shift what you know to be true for you.

Breastfeeding, in those first few weeks, can be so painful. However, with proper help and determination, breastfeeding can and hopefully will become one of the greatest gifts you can give to you and your baby. As Natalie's story shows, there are people out there who can support us with every aspect of discomfort we may be facing.

This can be really tough on us and our relationship with our partner. We have to trust the process and do what feels right for us. Sex may not be great at first. It takes a little while to get back into that groove. Working out is not easy. We remember where our body was and it's discouraging. We want to feel good. It's good to talk to our partner and let them know how we are feeling. We often want to retreat into ourselves and our negativity but that's the worst thing we can do. Most partners share the feeling of helplessness because they know their wife is hurting but they feel there is nothing they can do to help. They want to help.

All of this discomfort can weigh in to overwhelming feelings of sadness, anger, and even resentment. It's real and many women feel it. We don't talk about it as much as we should. With these cloudy, negative emotions on the lens of the soul, it's impossible to see the pure perfection of lives unfolding exactly as they are meant to unfold.

We have to build our community, we have to practice MAMAHH Moments so we are getting the self-care we need to get through this physical, mental, and emotional discomfort that is totally natural. Even though we all feel it, it doesn't make it any easier.

Disconnection. In the early months with a baby, the biggest thing we need that so many of us don't get is connection. When we are physically, mentally, and emotionally taxed, it's so difficult to connect to anyone. Our first response is to run and hide, but what would benefit our households and humanity more is focusing our energy on connecting during the tough times and remembering to celebrate the good times.

We need to connect with our partners during this time to take care of each other. We give our all to our babies and it's easy to go against each other. We feel shame for not knowing what to do. But it's natural for us to not know what to do, as parents parenting this new baby—whether it's our first or our fourth, each child is unique. We don't have all the answers but we are so afraid of failing. We are so afraid of failing that we try to appear like we have it all figured out. But now is the time to ask questions, connect with others, be a part of a supportive tribe, and not be afraid to ask for help.

Another reason connection is essential is because it's what our children feel. It's what makes them thrive when they feel that loving connection from us. If we are feeling disconnected from ourselves, our partner, our friends and family, we can't give our children what they need either. We are just beginning to understand how important our mental and emotional state is as parents and there are things we can do to improve it. When we lose that connection with ourselves, we aren't feeling love and compassion—and we are not able to give what we don't have. When we feel connected and filled up, we are able to say yes to the relationships and opportunities coming into our lives to help us blossom deeper into our soul self.

In the next section, we are going to share the tools Peaceful Mamas need to better handle all of these tough emotions and feelings that arise during pregnancy and motherhood. It's not about dwelling on all the negative things in parenthood and it shouldn't be about seeing them through rose-tinted glasses to make it seem like everything is perfect. Neither reaction is really productive.

What we need to hear more about is how:

- The negative, raw, intense feelings are real.
- Why our mental state is as important as our physical state.
- We all feel them as new moms, none of us is alone with these things.

There are tools for us to allow these feelings to pass through us with compassion so that we can make way for the good positive feelings on the horizon.

There are a number of proactive practices we can implement to make us better equipped to handle the waves of emotions that will ride in—starting with self-care and wholehearted living.

We are learning more and more that the way a Mama feels has lasting effects on her children. Children are resilient and can rewire, but the way they are treated early on leaves a lasting impression, one that they carry with them and will continue to ride up against until they are ready to understand them in their own time. They are learning how to love and be loved, and if a mother struggles with showing her child love the baby feels that. Just as the baby felt it in the womb, he feels it now in the flesh. Babies' brains are growing and rewiring and we want them to grow with the feeling of love. And when we love ourselves, we can fully embrace the beautiful act of wholeheartedly loving our children.

CHAPTER 5

THE SACRED AND TRANSFORMATIVE POWER OF MAMAHOOD

NATALIE

There is something sacred about becoming a Mama and nurturing children. And a Mama deserves awards and credits for all that she undertakes during her lifelong tenure as a mother. The act of parenting, mothering, and caring for the mental, physical, emotional, spiritual, digestive, and energetic health and well-being of another soul entitles the "position" of motherhood to reverence and respect. When we view our tasks as such, we are creating a highly valued and important career which deserves to be held in the highest esteem.

I use the term *career* to describe Mamahood because a job can sometimes imply that there is a beginning and an end, whereas a career almost seems infinite. Which describes Mamahood more appropriately. When you decide to bear children, or adopt or however you have consciously chosen (or not) to become a parent, you are undertaking an enormous responsibility. When you view it as sacred, as something that is more precious than diamonds and more delicate than a butterfly, then the choices you make reflect that care.

Your children will always reflect back to you the energy that you show them. For example, when I am feeling impatient, my children will mirror that back to me. So often I hear myself saying things like, "You just need to be patient, bud." And, then I think to myself, perhaps it is *I* who needs to be patient. Or I will hear myself saying, "You're just not making this fun." And, then I realize, oh shit. *I'm* the one who is not making this fun.

Of course, there are times when the mere idea of mustering up energy to make something fun seems damned near impossible, like at the end of a long day when attempting to get both children showered, teeth-brushed and pajamaed does not seem like fun at all. But that's when I need to lighten up. Be more present. Choose to chill and surrender.

Surrender is an awesome word. I love it. I have a pretty deep connection to the word because of personal experiences of having to completely surrender and just trust that a higher power would lead me where I needed to be. So, when I think about surrendering to my children, I think of it as letting go of whatever pre-conceived thoughts, emotions, or plans I had. I think about how unimportant my agenda really is and I often ask myself the question: "Will this really matter in five years from now?"

When we think of life from a grander view—as eternal—it is easier to release and surrender. Does it really matter if the children take an extra five minutes to get ready because they want to run around and play with one another? What could I be preventing? Perhaps a special bond between my boys.

"Every mother is giving an enormous gift to herself when she has a baby. We are given a gift to grow into who we are meant to be. Bringing a baby into the world helps us see ourselves in a new light and evolve into something greater than we even thought possible, something exquisite. In growing deeper into ourselves, we are giving our children a great gift. We are showing them how they too can live a life that is their own."

~ Lindsay

I want my children to have a close relationship with me, but equally as important, I want them to experience a special bond with one another. A lifelong bond that they cherish. And, the only way for that to happen is by creating memories, creating experiences, creating moments that bind them together. Times that are beloved and unique. Ones they can look back upon years later when they have children of their own and say "remember when…" and then share a laugh.

That type of bond is precious and holy. And, as a Mama, part of my responsibility is allowing space for that type of relationship to develop and then providing more opportunities to cultivate that brotherhood, enabling their bond to flourish.

It takes work. It takes persistence. It takes love, care, and authenticity to become the Mama you strive to be. And, as we have talked about in previous chapters, it is not going to happen all the time. It will be extraordinarily trying and challenging at times. You will feel like you have absolutely no strength inside of you by day's end, sometimes. But, remember this, you are powerful beyond belief, you are a warrior, you are immeasurably loving and you were chosen to be your child's or children's Mama! (Check out the book *Spirit Babies* by Walter Mackichen for more info.) What you decide to do with that immense gift is ultimately up to you.

We are all individuals and will therefore take on parenting and its responsibilities in our own unique way. The decisions you make could possibly reflect how you were parented, because we do what we see. We do what we hear. We do what we know...until we decide to change. If, in fact, we want to change. The choice is always and will forever be ours. Here are the questions that have inspired me:

- What kind of Mama do I want to be?
- How do I want to feel at the end of the day?
- How do I intend for my children and spouse to feel?

Although we can't control their actual feelings, we are ultimately in control of our answers to these private inquiries—and our answers can and do make a difference.

Oprah often quotes author and brain scientist Dr. Jill Bolte Taylor, who wrote, "Please take responsibility for the energy you bring into this space" after she experienced a massive stroke and tells the story of that experience. I often think about that quote because it resonates so truly for me. When I walk downstairs and my family is in the kitchen, I have the power to enter the room with love, excitement, and a laugh, or I can walk in and begin complaining of the loud noise and the fact that they woke me up. In an instant I have affected everyone's mood and their energy. Which one should I choose? That one simple decision could potentially alter the trajectory of the rest of the day.

The thing is that once we become a Mama, we sometimes feel like a part of us has disappeared. Perhaps we were once a major corporate powerhouse and now we are staying at home full time. Or maybe we decided to go back to work but our heart is not fully connected to our money-making job anymore. Maybe we were taking a leave of absence and during that leave we lost confidence, lost the faith that we are capable of separating ourselves from the title "Mama." These are all typical and understandable feelings. Just because we feel a certain way one day does not mean we will always feel or think that way though. It's called evolution.

I remember when I was pregnant with Jonah and I was teaching Pilates and a ballet barre class full time. I love teaching. My heart sings when I'm able to share my passions with other people and whenever I teach I am 100 percent committed and present to the moment and to my clients. I remember thinking to myself: what if after I have my baby something changes and I don't want to teach anymore, or don't think I can teach anymore?

So, I decided to write myself a letter. To the future version of myself. Here is a copy of that letter:

Dear future Natalie,

Congratulations! You're a Mama! I can't believe it. How do you feel?

I'm so curious to know how and when labor started. Where were you? Was it as painful as you thought, or worse? Did you get the epidural in time? Vaginal or C-section? Who delivered you? Was Lance able to drive you to the hospital? Or was he at work?

From what we've read, the baby blues is a common part of postpartum. Are you OK? Are you feeling depressed or let down? Whatever and however you are feeling is OK. But, let's make sure you are thinking clearly.

Let's talk about what's normal. Feeling hormonal, crying, moody, overwhelmed... all natural. Your life has just changed drastically...but it's for the best. Look at your new lil' nugget. How sweet is that face? How lucky are you to have Lance? He only wants what's best for you and baby. Cut him a little slack and remember what you heard a new father once say: "I feel helpless."

Don't make Lance feel that way. He doesn't deserve that. He would do anything in the world for you. He loves you unconditionally.

Remember that healing is a process. Your vagina, your uterus, your insides...they need time to heal. Be patient with yourself. You will get your body back. All in due time. Patience...it is a virtue. It is a moral goodness. Something, sometimes, difficult to attain because patience is not instant. You will not be skinny and tight instantly. But, you will be eventually. It took TEN months to gain the weight. So, it cannot possibly come off in a few short weeks. But, it will. You are determined and strong, but also realistic. Be realistic, be fair, be honest with yourself.

Breastfeeding is important to you and baby. Also, be patient. Remember it can take forty days to get it started. Get help if you need it. Ask Lance to call someone from La Leche League or a lactation consultant from the hospital. Do not suffer in silence.

Sleep. You need it. I know you are paranoid and scared and excited, etc. But, you need sleep. Ask Lance to watch the baby so you can sleep. Call your mom. Sleep when the baby sleeps. You have monitors for a reason.

Remember that everything is temporary. Your weight, your healing, the baby crying, the lack of sleep. A scheduled, structured life is ahead. It may just take a few months to get there.

Remember how much you love teaching. Your clients are so wonderful and support-ive. Go back to work. Even if it is for a couple hours a day, a few days a week. You will feel better. Surround yourself with other moms who understand and have been there. Your job, your clients, the studio are all important to you and make you feel good about yourself.

You have created a baby with your husband out of love. Don't lose that love for each other. Remember to hug and kiss and snuggle each other as much as you hug and kiss and snuggle your baby. Tell Lance how much you love him.

You are going to be OK!

I love you.

I read that letter on the way home from the hospital with Jonah and started crying because I was so happy that I had taken the time to honor myself like that. As we move through motherhood we evolve, we change, we go through a metamorphosis and fine-tune who we are and our life's purpose. Sometimes, actually oftentimes, as a result of becoming a Mama we are able to really prioritize what is important to us. It gives us perspective on what we want out of life. It is easy to get caught up in the day-to-day of diaper changes and feeding schedules. However, it is important to also take the time to perspectivize (my own word) your life. How can your talents, abilities and gifts evolve into something even more exquisite? You may not have the answer to that right now and that is totally OK! Just remind yourself and have the confidence in yourself that you can be, do, think, and become anyone you want.

LINDSAY

Every mother is giving an enormous gift to herself when she has a baby. We are given a gift to grow into who we are meant to be. Bringing a baby into the world helps us see ourselves in a new light and evolve into something greater than we even thought possible, something exquisite. In growing deeper into ourselves, we are giving our children a great gift. We are showing them how they too can live a life that is their own. As we embrace and accept our own uniqueness, we are modeling that way of living to our children. When we see each child with his or her own super soul different from our own and every other person on this planet, we can let go of our personal agenda and expectations of them and know their purpose in the world will be different from our own.

No two parents are the same just as no two children are the same. Yet deep within all of us is love. We connect within by doing the things that fill us up, which allows our light to shine out. I read this quote often because it describes what I am trying to convey here so well. You can let the word God be synonymous with whatever resonates with you—perhaps spirit, universe, light, creator, or source.

"Our deepest fear is not that we are inadequate. Our deepest fear is that we are powerful beyond measure. It is our light, not our darkness that most frightens us. We ask ourselves, Who am I to be brilliant, gorgeous, talented, fabulous? Actually, who are you not to be? You are a child of God. Your playing small does not serve the world. There is nothing enlightened about shrinking so that other people won't feel insecure around you. We are all meant to shine, as children do. We were born to make manifest the glory of God that is within us. It's not just in some of us; it's in everyone. And as we let our own light shine, we unconsciously give other people permission to do the same. As we are liberated from our own fear, our presence automatically liberates others."

—Marianne Williamson
From *A Return To Love: Reflections on the Principles of A Course in Miracles*

When we are following our own heart, doing what fills us up inside, we can give our children the full love, acceptance, and support they need to grow into their own unique selves. Too often we get caught up in our own agenda worrying of how things look to other people, getting ahead, that we can crush our children's spirit that is so bright and creative and wondrous. We do this when we are not in a conscious, mindful state but running on autopilot instead, as we get sometimes when we ourselves are lost.

"We want what we consider to be 'best' for our children, but in seeking to bring this about we can easily forget that the most important issue is a child's right to be their own person and lead their own life in accord with their unique spirit."

—Dr. Shefali Tsabary, Author of *The Conscious Parent*

How do we give our children the freedom to be their own person and lead their own unique life? That uniqueness is innate. It is within them just as it is within us. We honor it by honoring it within our own selves. Too many of us have become unconscious to our personal uniqueness, of what makes us special. We all have a gift to share. Yet, it's easy to lose sight of our own dreams, purpose and desires for our life. Perhaps because of others' agendas that were placed upon us—maybe from our own parents' unmet desires, cultural expectations, following someone else's path, or seeking unfulfilling materialistic things instead of the true desires of our hearts. Whatever it is or whoever may have influenced us away from the paths of our own hearts doesn't really matter. What matters is only how we choose to live right now. We have this moment to let go of those old agendas that don't serve us anymore. Our children, with their bright, courageous spirits, give us that inspiration. We want them to know they should follow that passion within them that we can see so vividly from the moment they come into our arms. Each child is different and unique and we can see it and feel it. Let's not crush that uniqueness. Let's embrace it by embracing it within our own selves.

"The greatest burden a child must bear is the unlived life of its parents."

—Carl Jung

We come into this world with a purpose that is unique to each of us. There is something within us this world needs. That is what makes our purpose unique, but it is connected to the rest of humanity too. I say this because our purpose is the way in which we serve others. Serving others is the ultimate way we can find the

happiness, fulfillment, and meaning we all desire in our life. We have the magical and miraculous ability to give something of ourselves to others that nobody else can. Too often, we lose sense of what this is.

Parenting has the incredible ability of unearthing our lost desires because parenting in itself is a great act of service. We are giving so much to our babies, especially in the early months of their life. We do everything for them and we are deeply connected to how they feel. It affects us on a profound level and we do everything we can to make them feel good. It may be the greatest act of service any of us face up until this point in our lives.

As we serve our babies, we feel good. Serving others is why we are here, and the act of being a parent gives us a glimpse into this. Yet, too many of us allow this to completely take over. We forget that we are not able to adequately serve others if we're not serving ourselves too. As we discussed in the last chapter, we need to fill ourselves up in order to serve others.

And as our children get a little older, as we move on from those early weeks, our priorities shift and we are able to spend longer chunks of time nurturing ourselves. We need to—it's mandatory. Not only because we love ourselves, but because we love our children, and the happier and healthier we are, the happier and healthier they will be too.

In the rest of these pages, we'll share how Mamas can reclaim their own lost spirits. How we can ignite ourselves and in doing so allow our children to live their lives as they are meant to live. Our planet needs more people following their hearts and leading with compassion and love. When we feel ourselves, we can have empathy for others. When we are disconnected and lost from ourselves, we can hurt another, but we are always hurting ourselves more when we hurt another. It causes us to put more armor on, preventing us from actually feeling, and further distancing us from ourselves. Being a parent lets us shed some of the layers we have built up because our children give us the pure unconditional love that we all need and desire. It allows us to forgive our past and create a bright future by living this new moment with intention and the highest energy of love, as our children do. Our children help us let go of what was and feel again now. But too many of us are unconscious to this transformative experience before us—which is why so much starts with a Peaceful Mama.

Are you ready? The following chapter is where Mama becomes MAMAHH in a single moment. With interwoven wisdom from our Peaceful Mama tribe of experts, we share the MAMAHH Moments, a cornucopia of creative ways in which you can reconnect with yourself, so you can connect with your children in a compassionate, loving, and empathetic way. The practices are designed to support you in giving your children what they need most, love, because it's radiating from your pores. It is within you. And the more you connect and grow into yourself, living your own purpose, you are serving others because you are giving something to the world that nobody else can.

Let's go, Mama!

CHAPTER 6

MAMAHH Moments Framework

Ahhh, we've arrived at the moments of truth! The relatively miniature practices that can create monumental change. The heart of the Peaceful Mama Movement—the MAMAHH Moments! Let's lay out the framework:

- **The Moment.** First we define this particular moment, including why we've found it to be important, how we make time for it in our day and how it's evolved from pregnancy, newborn stage, to right now. Our personal stories are interwoven here, in case our specific experiences may resonate with you, to offer extra insight.

- **The Facts.** Peaceful Mamas are grounded, so naturally we summarize the foundation and any research that backs this practice!

- **The Practice.** Next, we offer ideas for the practice, idea lists of actionable ways to incorporate these into your everyday routine.

- **Reflection Time.** Be inspired to get creative, Mama! You'll reflect and write out goals for your own practice. We offer questions to help you dive inside yourself and think about what is important to you, guiding you to write powerful statements of intention that can lift your and your family's life to a whole new dimension.

- **The Expert Excerpts.** You'll find these interlaced with our words, providing additional wisdom, support, and inspiration for your Peaceful Mamahood.

MOVEMENT

Movement means moving our body. It does not have to be a regimented routine or structure of any kind. However, movement should happen every day for our physical body to thrive. And, what better way to move your body than to thread exercise throughout your day?

Exercise is a phenomenal way to boost your immune system. "You need to be physically active during pregnancy. It has terrific benefits that are associated with a better pregnancy outcome and even shorter labors. It's a win-win for baby and for mom," says high-risk pregnancy expert Laura Riley, MD, spokeswoman for the American College of Obstetricians and Gynecologists (ACOG) and author of *Pregnancy: You and Your Baby.*

Not every exercise is safe to do during pregnancy. Exercises involving balance, like biking or skiing, or contact sports like soccer, can be risky during pregnancy. Around the fourth month your balance is affected. So that's when you don't want to do anything that will put your body in an unstable position, which is any exercise or activity that requires balance. Of course, consult with your doctor before you start any exercise program. Some women will not be able to exercise during pregnancy because of specific conditions or complications.

If you have never exercised before, pregnancy is not the time to start triathlon training. But that doesn't mean you have to spend nine months lounging around. Remember M is for movement. So, just make sure you are moving your body on the daily. Something as simple as taking a daily walk or going for a swim can do wonders for your pregnancy, and make you feel better as well. It can also help you combat the fatigue of pregnancy and help you sleep better at night. Whatever route you take, just make sure you listen to your body and begin slowly.

THE FACTS

According to the American Academy of Obstetrics and Gynecology, it's perfectly safe to exercise during your pregnancy as long as your doctor gives you the OK. They recommend that all women who have no complications with their pregnancies get "30 minutes or more of moderate exercise a day on most, if not all, days of the week," adding that the exercise can be anything you enjoy that doesn't risk abdominal trauma. They say that mobile Mamas have less risk of gestational diabetes, heart problems and even prenatal depression.

As a Yoga, Pilates, Stretch, Meditation, and Fitness Instructor, I am passionate about exercise. As soon as I could walk, my parents put me in dance classes, on ice skates, in the pool, on skis, and in sports. And although soccer was not my strong suit, at a very young age, exercise was a part of my life. It was never a chore or an obligation, it was just part of my normal routine, like brushing my teeth and going to school. And, as I grew up I became more interested in the dance side of exercise and less on the team sport side.

My parents encouraged me to follow my passion and to dance my way through high school, college and beyond. And, for me, it made my career choice quite easy. I continue to need and want exercise in my life because it makes me feel good. Not just physically, but mentally and emotionally too. Not everyone has that passion for movement, but no one can deny how much better they feel after a good sweat. Exercise and stress relief go hand in hand.

When you exercise, your body releases endorphins. Physical activity helps to bump up the production of these, your brain's feel-good neurotransmitters. I'm sure you've heard of a runner's high, but any form of exercise can contribute to this same feeling.

What I love about Yoga and Pilates is that they rehabilitate the physical body. They also have an element of connectedness to the mind, a focus on breath, and a whole-body approach. With that being said, we are not just physical bodies. We also need to rehabilitate the mind, body and spirit. An emotional rehabilitation.

Exercise takes care of it all. It is meditation in motion. After a challenging workout, you'll often find that you've forgotten the day's irritations and instead are able to concentrate only on your body's movements. As you begin to regularly shed your daily tensions through movement and physical activity, you may find that this focus on a single task, and the resulting energy and optimism, can help you remain calm and clear in everything that you do.

And, as a result, exercising will naturally improve your mood. How often do you walk into the gym or Yoga/Pilates studio in a foul mood or stressed out about life, your family, your job, but when you leave you have this sense of calm and new perspective? Regular exercise can increase

"Exercise can also improve your sleep, which is often disrupted by stress, depression, and anxiety. ... It can be 5 minutes, 10 minutes, 20 minutes... as long as we are successfully moving our body every day, we are boosting our happy hormone, serotonin. Whenever you consciously embrace Movement, you'll remember how Movement is an essential key to optimal vitality. Exercise is mental, physical, emotional, social, and spiritual therapy."

~Natalie

self-confidence and lower the symptoms associated with mild depression and anxiety. Exercise can also improve your sleep, which is often disrupted by stress, depression, and anxiety. All this can ease your stress levels and give you a sense of command over your body and your life. It can be as simple as going for a walk with baby, or doing a few squats, lunges, push-ups and gentle healing abdominal work. It can be 5 minutes, 10 minutes, 20 minutes... as long as we are successfully moving our body every day, we are boosting our happy hormone, serotonin. Whenever you consciously embrace Movement, you'll remember how Movement is an essential key to optimal vitality. Exercise is mental, physical, emotional, social, and spiritual therapy.

The Practice

Granted, this is all fabulous and useful information so far, but we understand when you are an expectant Mama or a new Mama, your availability physically, mentally and emotionally may not be the same as pre-conception. When you're a pregnant Mama, there will be days when you are too exhausted to exercise, especially in the first few months. Listen to your body—it is oftentimes smarter than you. And, that is OK! In fact, it's more than OK. It's natural, normal and healthy to listen to your body and what it is requesting of you. Perhaps there are days when you just want to lie around and watch TV. Go ahead and do that and then when you are feeling a little stronger, go for a walk around the neighborhood. If you are feeling lazy and unmotivated, sometimes just telling yourself that you are going to go for a 10-minute walk seems totally do-able.

So, set a small goal for yourself. If you are overly ambitious in your goal-setting you may end up doing no exercise at all. For instance, if you tell yourself that you will run three miles every day but you are feeling tired one day, you will easily talk yourself out of that lofty goal. Whereas, the 10-minute walk seems much more attainable.

With that being said, consistency is also important when you are exercising. Your body and muscles begin to atrophy in as little as 24 to 48 hours. So, if you aren't consistent with your exercise routine, it's almost like you are having to retrain your body and your muscles. However, when you are creating life in your body or have just given birth, then the stakes change. Your priorities are not about striving for the perfect body or getting into the best shape of your life. No one is saying that cannot or will not happen in the future, we are just suggesting that perhaps now is the time to be more gentle on yourself and your expectations. There is a lifetime of opportunity to run marathons and climb mountains, but this baby-making time and these postpartum days are precious and should be treated as such.

Fortunately, regardless of how your exercise routine changes while pregnant and postpartum, your muscles will remember. You just have to be diligent about reminding them. When choosing an exercise program, it's most important to find something you actually enjoy doing. If you hate running, but think that running is the only way to do cardio, then you're setting yourself up for failure. Not only will you despise running every time you go out for a jog, but you will come up with every excuse in the book to avoid running today. And, then today turns into tomorrow and the next day and so on.

But, if you LOVE to move and dance and feel like a ballerina, then perhaps a ballet barre class would be ideal. You will enjoy yourself while you are doing it. If you love to stretch and meditate then a yoga class is an appropriate choice for you. Or if you want a combination of stretch, strength, stamina and stability then try Pilates. The point is you want to set yourself up for success and choosing the right exercise regime will put you in the right direction.

Just like with diet and lifestyle, you must find a balance with your exercise routine. It's important to implement cardio, weight and strength training, and stretch. You shouldn't solely focus on one versus the other. Cardio doesn't have to be running or spinning, it can be anything that gets your heart rate up—a Zumba class or an exciting ballet barre class, or a simple walk around the block can do that for you. And, strength training doesn't have to be in the gym with 25-pound dumbbells.

Always keep in mind where you are in your pregnancy or postpartum and what is safe and recommended for you as your body changes. For example: because you should avoid any exercises that you have to do on your back after the first trimester, try some gentle standing pelvic tilts, seated belly breathing, or tightening abs, holding, then releasing, as good ways to keep ab muscles in top condition.

You can easily get your strength training in with a Pilates apparatus class because of the spring resistance it offers. Plus, it is low impact and gentle on your joints, unlike heavy weights where you can easily injure yourself. The resistance training also elongates your muscles, as opposed to heavy weights that give your muscles more of a bulky appearance. And, stretching doesn't have to be a yoga class, although it is an excellent way to increase your flexibility, you can stretch in a mat class or during your cardio class. The idea is, you want to find balance in your exercise regime, as well. Two to three days of cardio and two to three days of strength training is ideal. For detailed exercise routines, check out *Yeah Baby!* by Jillian Michaels, which provides an appendix filled with exercise routines, pictures, and related information.

From the *PeacefulMama.com* List of Recommended Reads:

Yeah Baby! The Modern Mama's Guide to Mastering Pregnancy, Having a Healthy Baby, and Bouncing Back Better Than Ever

by Jillian Michaels

Keep in mind that, while you are pregnant, your body is going through many changes. One of these changes is the production of the hormone relaxin. It is a hormone produced by the ovary and the placenta with important effects on the female reproductive system during pregnancy. In preparation for childbirth, it relaxes the ligaments in the pelvis and softens and widens the cervix. It also relaxes the ligaments in your entire body, tricking you into thinking that you are more flexible than you actually are. So, make sure that you do not injure yourself by overstretching. And, if you are not a fitness or yoga professional, please do not attempt poses without a qualified professional to help guide you and make sure you are being safe.

Additionally, postpartum Mamas, you should inform your instructors about the birth of your babe to ensure they can assist your modifications appropriately.

"Eat mindfully and nourish yourself."

~Natalie

Be gentle with your body as it heals. C-section Mamas and vaginal birth Mamas require special attention and should not just jump back into an exercise routine without the go-ahead from their midwife or OB and even still, they should take it slowly in the beginning. This is when Mamas are most eager to get back into their jeans, but it is also the time when they should respect the process of healing and not rush into an intense exercise program. You only get one chance to serve, protect, and honor your body in this lifetime. Be patient. Trust me, I know it's not easy. That's why the old adage "patience is a virtue" is so accurate.

And, remember, as with everything, there is a fine line between exercising and overexercising. Your body and muscles require opportunities to build and repair themselves. Listen to your body and remember, it is much safer to listen to your body when it is whispering than when it is screaming at you. The whispers are a gentle sign, whereas the screams are usually because injuries have already occurred.

We don't always lose weight on intense exercise routines or strict cleanses because of our stress hormone called cortisol. Restricting calories is stressful to the body, and it reacts by releasing cortisol. Cortisol is performance-enhancing in the short term, but if you somehow keep your body stressed for long periods, it creates havoc in your system and can cause you to hang onto weight in a type of survival mode. So, eat mindfully and nourish yourself during these tender times.

MOVEMENT IN A MAMAHH MOMENT

If you only have five minutes for exercise, what can you do? Any and all of these suggestions are generally safe for preconception, prenatal, and postpartum—always check with your trusted practitioner before engaging in any exercise routine:

- **Try a mini yoga session.** Lie in child's pose and reconnect to your breath, gently move into downward dog releasing any tension in your body and matching movement with your breath. Ease yourself into an alternating cat/cow position, feeling your spine elongate and your lungs fill with clean air.

- **Take a brisk walk around your neighborhood.** Walking is always a good choice to get your blood pumping and heart rate up. As you walk, focus on your breath. Is it shallow or are you taking long, cleansing breaths?

- **Exercise as you play with baby.** Once the doctor/nurse practitioner or midwife gives you the OK, feel free to incorporate some lunges and squats as you play with your baby, or add some push-up kisses—kiss baby every time you do a push up, placing baby in an easily accessible place to kiss!

- **Move with other Mamas.** Check out Meetup or connect with moms' groups to see what's available in your community. Moving with others makes it more meaningful and gives you accountability.

- **Remind yourself to move.** Set an alarm on your phone if that helps to remind you to stand, move around, or go for a walk.

Reflection Time

Phew! We understand that was a lot to take in, but we promise it'll be worth it. Take this time to check in with yourself and answer these questions honestly:

- What is your current level of fitness?

- Are you moving your body daily and what are you doing specifically?

- What are your goals and intentions for the preconception, prenatal, and postpartum phase?

Write these down. Sometimes the simple act of writing your goals down can help to align yourself with your goals and accomplish them. The moral of this chapter is—honor your baby and your body. There will be plenty of time in the future to focus on your personal fitness goals. For the time being, as you are growing a human being inside of you, or have just given birth, exercise with the intention of health in mind. Move every day and always make sure you are using your body safely, productively, and respectfully.

The Expert Excerpts

Why Movement Matters To New Moms

By Kathleen Haden

When you're a new mom, your sleep cycle is usually off, you are tired, and you have a lot to do. If you can incorporate a walk, dance, and/or do some yoga daily, your perspective on being a new mom will change. Movement helps increase endorphins that allow you to sleep better, change hormone levels, and increase your energy. Movement most of all will change the way you feel, improving your outlook on life when things are hard or tiring.

If you're a mom with a newborn, I'd encourage you to get up each day and move by stretching. Pick up your newborn and dance to your favorite music. Even though you are tired, try it and see how it starts your day off differently.

Looking back, I didn't take enough time to enjoy each day with my new baby. Our children grow up so fast, and each milestone should be celebrated. Moving and looking at things from a joyful heart will change your whole outlook. Enjoy each moment—and each movement—of each day!

Kathleen Haden has dedicated over twenty-five years to fitness training, Pilates, and massage therapy. She is a Master Pilates instructor trained by some of Joseph Pilates' original teachers. She is certified through Physical Mind Institute, Polestar, Balanced Body, and Pilates Method Alliance (PMA) and holds a BS in Kinesiology and Bio-Mechanics/Dance as well as an MBA in Marketing. She is also a Healer and Sound Therapist and the co-director of Good Vibrations Music Co. and Yoga Acoustics.

Let Life Move You!

By Andrea Riggs

Having been a new mother with twins and two-and-a-half-year-old Lucy, I know what it's like to feel homebound. But, you are never really homebound. I took the triple-jogger stroller out running every day, for my sanity and for fun. It is our freedom to get outside and move that helps us breathe in fresh air, feel our heartbeat increase, and feel alive and human again!

When Lucy was tiny, I would take her on walks and do fitness workouts at home. Once she was old enough, I took her to the gym daycare. I always ran a bit because it was easy. When my twins came along I stuck with running because everyone enjoyed being outside and they were all at my fingertips. I am flexible and resilient, even in choosing my workouts and movement. My advice for finding movement you love, while struggling with sleep deprivation and anything else going on in your life, is to move towards that which moves you. In a nutshell, do what you love. The only one who knows your body is you and you know it best. Be confident in what you do and who you are. No one knows what is best for you and your baby better than you. Your intuition, which I like to call "your gypsy spirit," is wiser than you know. When you feel you are ready to do yoga, or go on a brisk walk, or leave for thirty minutes and prancercise outside for a bit, do it. Your movement does not have to be hard core or anything specific.

Some of the best movement you can do after giving birth is exploratory movement, checking in and seeing what is going on. Your body has been through a lot. It is a machine and is meant to heal all on its own, as long as you give it what it needs. What does your body need? Lots of sleep and rest, movement, and amazing fuel that is high in nutritional density (i.e., fermented foods like kefir, kombucha, and sauerkraut), water from a natural spring that is high in minerals, sunlight, rest, laughter, relaxation, and movement.

We can be passionate and driven in all we do—in raising our children, in our work, and in our play. Yet when we learn to really love the journey and ride the waves is when we learn the art of fulfillment and being accountable in our own lives. Don't let your kids be a distraction or an excuse for you to not do what you want! Don't allow your life to take any other course other than the one you choose. Be intentional with your life and all you do, especially while raising your child(ren). You are worth it, so take ownership, take a nap when you need to, let go of what you must, be a yes, and come from a place of: *I am ready now*. These tips from Baptiste Yoga will take you far in life—I guarantee it.

Andrea Riggs is a certified Baptiste Yoga Instructor and has held a variety of global fitness certifications including, but not limited to, Certified Personal Trainer with NASM, TRX, AFAA and ACE group fitness, and multiple Zumba Fitness certifications. She was contracted as a choreography specialist with Zumba Fitness and traveled globally instructing elite Zumba Fitness Certified instructors. Andrea has been teaching for over a decade and continues to expand into new spheres and adventures. Her book is *Gypsy Living: How to Unleash Your Gypsy Spirit and Live Your Most Daring Adventure,* and her online guide program teaches others how to harness the tools laid out in her book so that our most daring adventure CAN become a reality. Alongside her husband-soulmate, she holds her most privileged role in life as a mother of three mini-gypsies.

The Wrap-Up on Movement

"Exercise activates the same part of your brain an antidepressant drug does, but it's free and natural and too many of us overlook it when our mood is down. Exercise is more than repetitive motion on a machine at a gym—there are so many other soulful ways to exercise that will make you actually want to get out and do it. Step out of your comfort zone and see what's out there...."

~ Lindsay

Movement is an essential component to my well-being. When I am feeling down, I can often attribute it to a lack of movement. Whenever I notice my outlook is cloudy or nothing seems to be going right, I often tell myself to get moving. Moving around always helps.

Movement is an immediate mood-booster for my children and me. I am always amazed at how much walking outside, turning on dance music, or doing a few yoga poses together lightens and brightens our days.

Too often we are caught up in the granular details of our day, our life, our experience. This is when getting outside is ideal. Movement helps shift our perspective, enabling us to zoom out from our current experience and see it instead with fresh, calm, and grateful eyes. It helps our bodies just feel good! And that, in turn, helps our mind clear and our heart feel lively again.

After we have a baby and even towards the end of pregnancy, our ability to move our bodies freely may be limited. As someone who has had C-sections, I have to take it slowly. But movement always helps—even with the recovery.

When I had my first C-section, I was still so shocked by it all and tired from the experience that I didn't get out to move around until almost twenty-four hours after the surgery. This felt right at the time. With my second, I knew I needed to be moving faster than that. With the help of the nurses, I got up and took a walk as soon as I could, about twelve hours after the surgery. It definitely helped my recovery. The more I moved around, the better I felt.

When I think back to those first difficult movements after the surgery and the discomfort I felt throughout my whole body and where I am now, running most mornings—it's clear that the body heals in amazing ways. I'm grateful to say I actually ran a marathon a few months before writing this!

We'll all observe our personal milestones as we heal from carrying a baby and delivering a baby. It's different for each of us and we have to listen to our bodies. But on a day-to-day basis, it's important to remember that *even a little movement helps*. It's gradual and by taking little steps, know that soon you'll be where you desire to be.

Movement is healing. We are meant to be moving our bodies. It's good for us and our children. We see how natural it is in our children. They are always moving. Even as they are watching a show, they are jumping, standing, and getting into yoga positions without even knowing it. They remind us that however we can incorporate movement into our day, the better we are.

Gradually, step by step, we can strengthen by moving our body in a way that feels right for us. Getting the practice started early on, even during pregnancy, has a lasting impact as our children grow. It helps them see how important movement is too—especially as they grow and lose a bit of those natural desires to move that they had when they were young.

Keep exercise as a goal to reach toward. Its benefits are astonishing. Exercise activates the same part of your brain an antidepressant drug does, but it's free and natural and too many of us overlook it when our mood is down. The reason many of us have a hard time doing it is we haven't found a way to exercise that is right for us. Exercise is more than repetitive motion on a machine at a gym—there are so many other soulful ways to exercise that will make you actually want to get out and do it. Step out of your comfort zone and see what's out there.

So get moving, Mama! And see how good it makes you feel and how much calmer your baby is too.

AFFIRMATIONS

The way we speak to ourselves is important—and it's even more important as we become mothers. We hear this all the time in many different ways from some of the greatest scholars: "What we think, we become," said the Buddha. "I think therefore I am," said René Descartes. "Whether you think you can, or you think you can't—you're right," said Henry Ford. One of my favorites is a quote spoken by Henry David Thoreau's character in a famous play about his life. It's about being you: "Be yourself—not your idea of what you think somebody else's idea of yourself should be."

Applying these truths is easier said than done. We have to affirm the good, but we must first be aware of what we are thinking and take responsibility that we create the thoughts that create our world. In her insightful Ted Talk following her massive stroke, brain scientist Dr. Jill Bolte Taylor challenges us to pay attention to our self-talk and take responsibility for what we're thinking. She shares how an emotion like anger takes only ninety seconds to run through our body, to be felt in our physiology. Yet, we may feel anger for a whole day, a week, for years even as we rethink the thought that caused the anger (either consciously or not). We can respond differently to triggers; we don't have to keep re-experiencing these negative thought patterns. We'll get into how we do this more deeply in the next section.

THE FACTS

In motherhood, it's too easy to get caught up in negative self-talk. We feel like a failure and a hero from one moment to the next. We can easily get into a negative thought pattern of thinking we're not made out for this parenting thing. Or we think we're the only one who is struggling. We must remember that in every moment we did the best we could with the awareness and tools that we had at that time. Beating ourselves up about a past mistake serves nobody and does nothing other than take away from our present moment to start fresh.

We can pay attention to our inner dialogue. Negative self-talk is felt by our children too. They feel our energy—positive and negative. Research indicates that as we hold our babies, their heartbeats actually start to mimic our own. We have to become more aware, then we can make a shift. When we become mothers, it's more important than ever to recognize how we are speaking to ourselves, because the way we talk to ourselves is how we talk to our children. We don't even need to say a word. Our nonverbals speak volumes and our little children soak this up. In the wise words of Peggy O'Mara, "The way we talk to our children becomes their inner voice."

We can shift our thought patterns. When we become more aware and curious about our thoughts, we can choose to think and feel differently. The meditation teacher Sharon Salzberg puts it so beautifully: "Dedicating some time to meditation is a meaningful expression of caring for yourself that can help you move through the mire of feeling unworthy of recovery. As your mind grows quieter and more spacious, you can begin to see self-defeating thought patterns for what they are, and open up to other, more positive options." In other words, when negativity and fear-based thinking is taking over, we can recognize it, and choose a loving, positive thought that lifts us up. We shouldn't be against our own self and so many of us are.

We can choose self-compassion. When we are against ourselves, we're listening to fear-based thinking that is telling us to feel ashamed, resentful, and fearful. It's easy to let others speak this way to us too. When we are not in control of that negative spiral of thinking, that's when we know we need compassion. Often this begins with communicating our truth and respectfully asking others to speak with us in empowering ways. Not only does this help us, but it is an essential skill to model for our children. As Brené Brown reminds us, "Compassion is not a virtue—it is a commitment. It's not something we have or don't have—it's something we choose to practice."

One way to proactively plant more positive thinking into our heads is through affirmations. When we take time to affirm our strengths and the positives about who we are and what is ahead and right before us, it makes our moments better. We plant the seeds of more positive thinking and awareness, even when negative thinking creeps in.

Moms are susceptible to negative thinking. We are giving so much to our babies we often have little left for ourselves. We need to practice self-compassion, and to confidently choose love. We will lose it at times. Whether sinking into a depression or raging out in anger, both emotions rise from a dark place that makes us believe we are the only person who doesn't deserve compassion. We all deserve compassion. Challenge yourself to become curious, ask questions when we begin to feel badly. Sometimes the act of giving them attention in a kind way helps them pass. Next, we can try an affirmation practice.

Affirmation is the action or process of affirming an idea that you would like to see expressed in your world. We can choose to affirm negative or positive things in our life by the words we use. It comes from our imagination, which is such a powerful tool. Are we using our imagination or our thinking to resolve a problem or magnify it? We have to be aware of our thinking first, then we can change it.

Thoughts themselves are neutral. Take, for example, *"my son is having a meltdown."* Next comes emotion, like frustration or anger in this example. We may think, *"why does he always spill?"* or *"why me?"* These are beliefs, which can have a positive or negative charge. With awareness, we can recognize the beliefs *before* we choose to act or not to act on them. We can create some space between the experience and how we respond. We can choose a loving response rooted in a new positive belief, such as *"he's doing the best he can"* or *"let's turn this into a positive by cleaning it up together."*

As Mamas doing our very best, we shouldn't be against our own selves. Yet, many of us have an inner critical voice that has taken over. That judgmental voice serves a purpose: to keep us safe. It's primal and within all of us. But it doesn't have to control our life! With awareness, we can simply say no to that voice and choose to listen deeper.

There is a kinder, more positive core in every person and situation. But we don't always accept or even hear it. We may have gotten accustomed to being unkind to ourselves, to not seeing the positive in what we are experiencing. What if we treated ourselves the way we would treat a close friend or loved one? What if we reframed our situation to see the good in it? What if we asked the question, what am I meant to be learning here when we are challenged, instead of asking why me? It's easy to think the way we always thought. Or the way others told us to think about ourselves . . . but not for long, Mama! We've missed out on too much. It's time to step out of the safe zone, and choose courage over comfort. It's time to be vulnerable because that is how growth takes place.

> *"Vulnerability is at the core, the center,*
> *of meaningful human experiences."*

— Brené Brown, Ph.D., LMSW

We've all become so afraid of failure that we've felt it was easier to sit back, watch, and judge rather than step in, try, fail, and try again. Whether we like it or not, parenting puts us out there, into the arena, failing time and again and well out of our comfort zone. The thing is, we can't give up on parenting. Our kids are there waiting for us, depending on us, and learning from us, and we have to get back up. We can't quit like we may have done with other things that have been difficult throughout life. That is why parenting is the most challenging yet rewarding thing we can ever do.

We're not meant to be perfect at it. We're meant to grow through our parenting experiences into who we are meant to be. Where we "fail," we grow. One way to help us through the messy imperfection that is parenting is to be kind and compassionate to ourselves through the process.

So how do we stay centered, kind and compassionate
to ourselves during the messiness that is parenting?

Affirmations are just one of the tools to help us stay more centered. Our thoughts become things and that becomes obvious when we become parents. We can see how the things we think, and the energy that exudes from the thing we think, deeply affects those around us, especially our children. It affects their mood, behavior, and how they see the world. They are learning how to interact with themselves and others by what we model. When we are in a negative, reactive thought pattern and they see this time and again from us, they are learning to think this way, too.

We know now this impact of our thinking and being on our children starts in utero. Our babies feel what we feel. It's up to us to be responsible for our own thoughts and to challenge the beliefs that no longer serve us. We must remember this does not mean we will feel good all the time. We are human and we make mistakes, poor choices, and will feel all the emotions. In parenting especially—since we are often sleep deprived and/or overwhelmed—it becomes that much easier to falter.

It's more about how we treat ourselves when we falter or have tough moments. The sooner we recognize the negative mind chatter, the sooner we can flip the switch. We can actively choose to be kind and compassionate to ourselves for feeling this way. We can look to one of the tools in our belt to think differently and change our outlook. Affirmation is one of these tools.

When we look back at our own childhood experiences, it's easy to sit back and judge how our own parents raised us. And maybe even blame our current behavior on past experiences. But those things only exist in our head. We have to let go of the past by looking upon it with love, knowing our parents did the best they could with the tools they had. Taking negativity from our past into the present does only one thing—it prevents us from enjoying positive experiences in our present.

When we become parents ourselves, we often develop more compassion for our parents. Instead of judging our parents for their actions and having some resentment, we can simply say they did the best they could. And we can bring gratitude into this moment. Gratitude that we have more awareness and the tools to do better. Gratitude is the gateway to joy.

We want to have as many tools as possible to be our best. And we have to remember that our best changes moment to moment and day to day. The first step is to accept ourselves where we are. Affirmations help to ground us and give us a positive refresh to refocus our thoughts and beliefs. They help to bring us back to our intentions and away from any negativity that distances us from our present experience. Affirmations bring us back to center. And a centered state is the best way to handle the inevitable ups and downs of parenting.

Parenting calls us to step out of our comfort zone and embrace vulnerability. As Brené Brown says, "Vulnerability is the birthplace of innovation, creativity, and change." So, if affirmations are something that are new to you and make you a little uncomfortable, we challenge you to just give them a try. We have to be creative and open to change if we want to grow ourselves and be better for our children.

Affirmations help us focus and reframe our experience so we are creating a new story for ourselves, one in alignment for who we want to be. It's easy to be led astray and get caught up in negative thinking. As we said earlier, our thoughts create our world. Affirmations are one positive way to design our world in alignment with our intention and purpose.

LIFE-"AFFIRMING" CONVERSATIONS WITH A DOULA

The birth of a baby is a beautiful milestone in our own life, our family's life and equally as important, our newborn's life. It is considered the baby's first "experience."

Did you know that a newborn baby's brain fires neurons and, through synaptic pathways, wires together based on these crucial and precious first experiences? In other words, the actual birth and welcoming of the newborn into the world is an invaluable opportunity to provide warmth and love with gentle modalities and peaceful touch/sounds/environment.

Our Peaceful Mama Expert Zeresh Altork, doula, childbirth educator and counselor, shares: "A fetus/newborn is programmed to behave in certain ways and consequently expects a sequence of events to occur during and after birth to ensure his survival. The hormones of a natural birth encourage a positive and powerful experience."

Zeresh goes on to say that when a newborn is able to experience an unmedicated vaginal delivery, there are natural and powerful hormones released to help both Mama and baby. Ideally, a newborn is welcomed into the world with the assistance of his own birthing reflexes as well as his Mama's instinctual, spontaneous, and self-guided pushes, gently ejecting from the womb into loving hands, and immediately placed onto Mama's bare chest for skin-to-skin contact.

Our expert notes that this experience tends to be more available—and made a priority—when you have built a heart-centered, experienced, and well-qualified birth team, which views you as a powerful, capable woman who has strength beyond belief. We couldn't agree more!

There are multiple benefits to both Mama and baby when the cord is kept intact. Researchers have found that keeping the umbilical cord of a newborn intact with a goal of five minutes, or longer if the cord is still pulsating, may lead to better health benefits for the baby.[6] The umbilical cord delivers oxygen and food from a mother's bloodstream, via the placenta, into the baby's blood to provide nutrients. Babies whose cords are left intact at birth are less likely to have iron deficiencies later on in life. Additionally, minimizing external stimuli, while baby experiences skin to skin on his mother's chest, in what midwife and author of *Gentle Birth Choices,* Barbara Harper, call's "the sanctuary," helps give the baby a chance to express all his reflexes and for his brain to create healthy new neuropathways.

In the sanctuary of the mother's chest, the baby hears her heartbeat, smells her, is able to gaze up to her face, and feels her warmth, and most importantly her love and protection, which allows him to then express his natural reflexes and innate instincts. It creates a beautiful ripple effect and enables his brain to think: "I am in the right place, I am loved, I am safe." That becomes the building blocks for the way he will live his life. These are, in effect, *baby's first affirmations.*

No matter how much we plan, we don't know what type of birth our child will have. We share this information not to produce guilt or fear, just so you are informed. A traditional hospital experience may not make these types of experiences the norm. If you did not have this type of experience with your babe, please don't dismay: you still can…on the energetic level…via a process known as "revision," by re-envisioning in full technicolor the moments after your baby's birth as you wished they had been. It can be emotional and when deep-rooted emotions surface and you need help processing them, always seek the support of an experienced counselor. Yet we've found that the sheer act of revising can be profoundly healing for Mama and child. And if we didn't experience this with our Mamas, we can even do so from our own perspective as a newborn, sensing in our mind's eye that skin to skin with our Mama and re-imagining our very own first-ever, nonverbal affirmations as having been: "I am in the right place, I am loved, I am safe." And we can actually transmit that feeling of safety to our child in any place and at any time in their life.

"These first experiences set up the foundation for how a new human being will face his whole life. But our wise and loving doula reminds us that, whatever the birth experience is, we are also designed to overcome, to learn and grow, and create new neuropathways. There are steps a mother can take to help her newborn (or older child) and herself overcome separation and rough beginnings."

~Natalie & Lindsay

Zeresh also emphasizes that Peaceful Mamas need to be prepared to ask for what we want even as we stand supported by our dream A-team. For example, we can be misinformed and coaxed into thinking we "need" synthetic hormones (as in Natalie's first birth) or other interventions that could end up causing more harm than good. We want every Peaceful Mama to be empowered with all types of tools and information available so that we are prepared to take a stand in alignment with our own personal beliefs (whatever those are) and tap into our intuition when the time comes for labor, birth and delivery. Know the facts, know your options, and trust yourself when creating this first experience for your child.

These first experiences set up the foundation for how a new human being will face his whole life. But our wise and loving doula reminds us that, whatever the birth experience is, we are also designed to overcome, to learn and grow, and create new neuropathways. There are steps a mother can take to help her newborn (or older child) and herself overcome separation and rough beginnings. In other words, we understand that sometimes we are put in situations which challenge our ideals, and when this happens we know and trust that we can repair a challenging birth experience.

Doing a lot of skin to skin as soon as possible after a difficult birth experience is one of the simplest and most powerfully healing thing a new Mama can do with her baby. Additionally, therapeutic storytelling, role playing, remembrance baths, as well as speaking with a counselor experienced in birth trauma can be very healing for both Mama and baby/child. In many births, the interventions and disruptions to the birth process that occur are not only unnecessary but harmful. In some cases, interventions and separations are inevitable and necessary, but these can be done gently too, and as mentioned, there are ways to help both mother and baby overcome, and even prevent those difficulties. For example, if a mother is faced with the need to have a C-section, researching what a gentle C-section is and preparing for that is also a wonderful way to welcome her baby into this world. Just knowing this information empowers us! It is much easier to face life with positivity and ease when the first experiences are loving and gentle ones.

But what if a mother's birth doesn't go the way she hoped or expected, and the birth wasn't just difficult, but traumatic? It is important to note that in some cases recovery from traumatic childbirth may be especially difficult, possibly triggering postnatal depression. However, perinatal depression can occur at any time during pregnancy and postpartum and can have a particular cause, or can appear to come out of nowhere and without an apparent cause. If you are feeling down and not quite like yourself for a period lasting more than two weeks, or you are experiencing recurring fearful thoughts, know it is not your fault, and reach out to your care provider. There are also specific resources like www.2020mom.org, www.hmhb.org, and therapists that provide support specific to the needs of moms. If you find yourself feeling depressed or out of control, reach out for help, and know that there are resources, there is nothing to be ashamed of, and you are not alone! For more information on the subject of perinatal depression and a very informative documentary, visit www.darksideofthefullmoon.com.

"When we realize the importance of that first experience, we are able to help establish a foundation for a secure, loving, and happy new human being," Zeresh says. "We can all agree that we want our babies and ourselves to feel secure, loved and happy! This begins and continues with a strong Mama/baby bond."

Zeresh Altork, M.Ed., CD, CCE, CLC, BHC, is a mother, and is certified as a: doula, hypno-doula, lactation counselor, childbirth educator, and hypnosis for birth educator. She has been a doula since 2008 and has supported over 250 couples on their journey to parenthood. She has a Master's degree in Counseling and over fifteen years of counseling experience. Since 2014 she has been organizing and interpreting waterbirth workshops in Spain for midwife Barbara Harper, founder of Waterbirth International.

Healing Affirmations for Mama and Baby

One of the ways we can help ourselves and our babies is to practice positive affirmations during pregnancy, delivery, and immediately postpartum. Affirmations can include:

During pregnancy:

"I am strong and capable."

"I trust and nourish my body and baby with love."

During labor:

"My body is an amazing piece of machinery and knows exactly how to birth my baby."

"Baby and I are working together to make this experience beautiful." "I am at ease."

And, postpartum:

"I love you."

"Thank you for choosing me to be your Mama."

"You are safe."

"You are loved."

"You are amazing."

"You are my miracle."

"I respect and honor you."

These affirmations are for both Mama and baby. Regardless of how your labor and delivery unfolds, remember this: you are the creator of your own joy and happiness. Decide to be happy and the heart expands exponentially.

THE PRACTICE

"Affirmations allow you to design and then develop the mindset (thoughts, beliefs, focus) that you need to take any area of your life to the next level."

—Hal Elrod

- **When to do affirmations.** We ideally want to practice affirmations both at a set time each day, as well as call on them as needed throughout the day. Having a ritual or set time when you practice helps create the habit. Mornings are a great time because it helps you set the tone for your day and create a positive launching point. Another good time is in the evenings before bed. As a new Mama, evenings and mornings are blurred. This change in schedule—while it can take a lot out of us—creates a lot of time for self-reflection. We are up at different times during the night and throughout the day alone feeding our baby. Affirmations can also be combined with our many ritualistic activities throughout the day, whether it's diaper changing, feeding, or baby nap times. Paste them on your mirror or on your fridge—wherever you'll see them and be reminded to say them. (You'll read more on this from our experts!)

  You just have to find a time that works for you. You only need a few minutes. As with anything, you just have to keep at it. Once the habit is formed, you prioritize time for it because you look forward to it. We assure you that it won't be long before you feel the positive impact of this practice. You'll find negative thoughts don't spiral into whole days of negativity because you're able to more quickly recognize when your thoughts no longer serve you, and you can bring yourself back to the mindset you desire. You begin to live in a more centered, grounded state.

- **How to choose affirmations.** You can develop affirmations for any area of your life. It's good to write them out or type them. You'll find it becomes a living document. You will revise, edit, add and refocus your list as life moves, changes and evolves within you. I keep them in a great self-organization app called Trello. I have it on my computer and as an app on my phone. I can pull it up anytime I need a lift. As you practice affirmations more, you will remember some of them by heart. There may be one that you turn to all day long, repeating to yourself whenever you need to get centered.

  This is where creativity comes in. Only you know what you want to affirm in your life. You can have one or a few or many. You can use affirmations however serves you best. As Hal said, you are using them to design your own thoughts, beliefs and focus. Sometimes we run on autopilot. It's this mode of living where we don't think we have control of our own thoughts. Maybe we are so caught up in filling the needs of others that we have lost sense of our own needs. This can easily happen to us as parents. Affirmations help us refocus and find clarity on what is important—which, in turn, helps bring us back to center.

You see, we can't give and give to others without feeling filled up ourselves. Affirmations are one tool to help us fill ourselves up so we can give more to others. And especially when we're a new Mama, we have to give a lot to our newborn who needs us for everything. It's essential that at this time, more than ever, we have tools to give back to ourselves.

Reflection Time

Grab a journal and get ready to fly, Mama! We're about to share a few "starter ideas" for creating your own affirmations. A simple one to start is *"I am enough"* or *"I have everything I need, want, desire and more."* Repeating this inwardly helps us remember that within us we have everything we need and we are doing the best we can right now. This helps us let go of comparison and guilt and trust we can handle whatever comes our way. Here are some more:

- Start with "I am…" and write a word that captures the essence of *how you want to feel* (even if you don't feel quite that way yet, with practice you will!).
- I am peace.
- I am loved and loving.
- I am a radiating center of peace and love.
- I am worthy, deserving and capable of…. (fill in with whatever you desire)
- I am whole.
- I am strong and able.
- I can do all that is needed to do today.
- Peace begins within me.
- I choose love.

Mama, you deserve to feel whole and free and at peace. This is why it's good to set affirmations for all areas of life (Health, Fitness, Career, Self-Development, Spirituality, Marriage, Social, Career, Parenting and Quality of Life). We know that when any one area of our life is lacking or we are feeling unfulfilled, this negatively impacts all of the other areas. Even the areas that seem to be going really well are not whole when other areas are hurting. Eventually, you can move toward setting intentions in all of the areas of your life.

Start with one to focus on. Small steps. Here's an example of questions you could ask yourself for health and fitness: Remember a time when you felt really strong and healthy in your body. What did it feel like? What were you wearing? What were you doing? Think about feeling that way again. What do you see? How does it feel? What are you doing and eating and how are you moving to feel this way?

Get really clear about what you want. Then create an affirmation.

As we suggested earlier, it's good to start it as "I am" or "I choose" or "I feel" and add the word that you envision for yourself. And then add an action to it for how you are moving toward that every day. Here are some examples of this:

- I am fit…I make time every morning for moving my body with a jog outside or yoga or walking my baby in the stroller.
- I am centered…I live in awareness and bring myself back with kindness whenever I stray from positive thinking about myself and others.
- I choose love…I see everyone as doing the best they can. I accept my experiences as they come and see the good in them.

For more ideas on affirmation, check out the website of Louise Hay, *LouiseHay.com*.

AFFIRMATION DOS AND DON'TS

- **Do:** Feel free to get creative with your affirmations! When creating personalized affirmations, be clear and keep them positive.
- **Don't:** Use negative verbs and adjectives. For example, do not say: "I don't want to feel stressed or angry with my children today." Instead say: "I am peaceful, calm and compassionate to myself and my children." Our minds do not understand the negative.
- **Do:** Always try to stay in the positive tense, using phrases like: "I can, I am capable of, I trust, I have faith, I believe," etc. as opposed to staying in the negative vibration of words and phrases like "I don't want, I can't, I will not, I never," etc.
- **Don't:** Make your affirmations unbelievable. Sometimes I will say, "Even though it is hard for me to believe right now, I trust that everything will work perfectly in accordance with divine right timing." That way, I don't feel like I am lying to myself. It is important that we make sure that we resonate with what we are saying and that it rings true on some level with our internal belief system. Otherwise, affirmations will not "work" for you. I say "work" because things only work when you believe that they can work.
- **Do:** Try this one! In the shower (morning or evening) close your eyes, allow the water to cascade over you and chant, "I am washed by the waters of forgiveness. My heart is embraced by love." This is one of Natalie's all-time favorite quotes from the book *Spirit Babies* by Walter Makichen.

MORE EXPERT EXCERPTS
MAKING AFFIRMATIONS HABITUAL

By Cathy Cassani Adams, LCSW, CPC, CYT

Affirmations are an opportunity to live an examined life, to recognize what is happening in the moment and notice what's working. It's very easy to get caught up in what's not working—our brains are trained to notice and attend to problems. It's a mental practice (literally like exercise for the brain) to notice what is good, to recognize what sustains us and what we are doing well. For me, affirmations are similar to gratitude—to recognize, vocalize, journal about, and just appreciate what is right. When I'm with my kids, I do my best to look them in the eye, hold their hands, really attune to them when I'm with them. And when I'm on my own, I practice enjoying time to myself, recognizing that being alone allows me to be better when I'm with my kids. My most common affirmation is:

"It is my responsibility to take care of me, and to take responsibility for the energy I bring to every situation."

Of course, I ask for help, and of course I don't do this perfectly; but in the end, I get to choose how I react and respond, and to me that's empowering.

Make affirmations a part of your daily routine. When the baby is crying, it helps to have a phrase you say to yourself. When the baby is sleeping, make it a point to journal some of your joy. Before you go to bed list five things that made the day special, even if it seemed like a complete disaster. Learn to take deep breaths while holding or feeding the baby, creating a kind of meditation during the most seemingly mundane times. If you build affirmations into your routine, it makes them habitual and develops a sense of harmony that will sustain you through the repetition and challenges.

Cathy Cassani Adams, LCSW, CPC, CYT, is a self-awareness expert focused on parenting and the personal empowerment of women and young girls. She's a licensed clinical social worker, certified parent coach, certified elementary school teacher, certified yoga teacher, and she's a professor in the Sociology Department at Dominican University. She's also the author of several books and co-host of the podcast *Zen Parenting Radio*.

The Art of Affirming Your Worth

By Julie Reisler, Life Designer®

As a mom of two, back to back, it was beyond exhausting. I developed an auto-immune condition and I'm clear that it was in part because of the stress, the shortage of sleep, and the lack of self-care. I wish I had used more affirmations to notice and affirm what I was doing well. We are often so tough on ourselves, using language about ourselves that we wouldn't use with our worst enemy! Being kind to your mind and affirming what's working will change what you focus on, since what you focus on expands.

> *"Be open, loving, accepting and kind to yourself, first and foremost. You are a badass Mama . . . creating sacred beings to help make this world a more inspiring place. Thank you for who you are..."*
>
> *~Julie*

Remember to be kind to your mind, body and soul. You just created an entire human being—we can't quite comprehend what it takes for our bodies to be able to do this. Allow time for just you, even if it's a ten-minute moment locked in the bathroom (did that all the time). I gave myself "time outs" often, knowing that even a three-minute moment to breathe, pound my pillow, suck in the lavender oil I never use, or phone a friend for a quickie check-in… always paid off. And, if/when you do lose it with your child or children, forgive yourself. You are human. You are meant to make mistakes, grow and learn. Lastly, I'd invite you to see your kiddos as your biggest teachers. I can assure you, my duo has taught me way more about myself than any master's degree program. Be open, loving, accepting and kind to yourself, first and foremost. You are a badass Mama (I know, because you are reading this book) and you are creating sacred beings to help make this world a more inspiring place. Thank you for who you are and for taking on the most challenging life trek and journey known to humankind.

Julie Reisler, a Life Designer® with a master's degree in Health and Wellness Coaching, is the author of *Get a PhD in YOU*, Host of *The You-est You* podcast, and the CEO of Empowered Living LLC, a Life Design Coaching and Personal Development company. She is on the faculty at Georgetown University in their coaching program and works with individuals and groups both privately and in the workplace. Julie is all about helping her clients to design a life they love through powerful one-on-one coaching, group coaching sessions, and inspirational speaking engagements.

The Wrap-Up on Affirmations

Hi Mama, Natalie here to wrap up. I love doing affirmations. For one, I have an active imagination. My mind can organize, strategize, evaluate, and analyze all at the same time. And, sometimes that can be exhausting. In an effort to slow my mind down, breathe with more ease, regulate my heart rate, and feel more centered, I focus on one to two affirmations allowing me to find my instant peace. To help myself believe my affirmations are true, I start my practice by saying things that I absolutely believe. For example, "I am a Mama." There is really no debate there; I gave birth to two children whom I care for daily. That clearly makes me a Mama. I can also confidently say that "I am here." Which, wherever I am, is true. But, saying this automatically brings awareness to where I am and who I am with, gifting me and whoever I am with a gentle reminder to be and stay present.

A wonderful tip about affirmations from Hal Elrod is to add the words "I am committed to becoming" before an affirmation if it initially seems like a stretch. For example: "I am a *New York Times Best-Selling Author* multiple times over" is slightly far-fetched today since, as I am writing this, the book is yet to be published. However, "I am committed to becoming a *New York Times Best-Selling Author* multiple times over" sounds much more realistic. I could buy that. The key is making sure you are creating affirmations that resonate with you on multiple levels. Incorporate feelings into each of the words you choose. What is it you want to feel? Make sure you always say (clearly) what it is you want and refrain from saying things you DON'T want. Your affirmations will evolve just as you do. And, it is pretty spectacular when you are at a point in your mindfulness when you catch yourself spiraling and can instantly bring yourself back up with a few spot-on affirmations. Our tendency as human beings is to resist change and do what is comfortable and easy. Having children challenges this on every level and takes us out of our comfort zone. When we're uncomfortable, we may resort to old stories and negative thought patterns that don't help us in the present.

"Who's in charge, the thinker or the thought?"
—Susan David

Take the first brave step and use affirmations to create a new story for yourself, with thoughts in alignment with your desires. Allow affirmations to help you be more intentional and evolve in a positive way to who your soul dreams to be. It's quiet but that voice is there. Create the time to reflect on the prompts above, listen, and write out your desires. Be aware, curious, and compassionate with yourself as you create your new story—one with intention. Take time to be, receive, and give thanks for all the positive energy that exudes as you live completely and in harmony with your true values and desires.

MINDFULNESS

There is one thing that has become my greatest tool in parenting. It's not a discipline technique, strategy, or piece of gear. It actually has little to do with my children at all. It's all about me and it has the single greatest positive impact on my relationship with my children, their behavior, and our interaction together. It's mindfulness.

For me it's not just mindfulness, but something I call Positive Mindfulness that is the greatest tool we can have not just in motherhood, but in life. Positive Mindfulness is being aware and accepting of what is without judgment and with kindness and compassion. Being positive is courageously choosing to see the goodness in what is happening and remembering that any negative feelings are created by me and I can choose differently. Peace happens from this place when I am accepting what is with compassion and a trust that it is all part of my perfect path—which is unique from every other person on this planet. To me, it is the comparison of our own path to others as well as being lost in our own expectations of what could have been or should have been that makes positive mindfulness hard to adopt. But, it is from this positive, accepting mindset, that we can see even the hardest things in our lives through a new lens. I ask, "What am I meant to learn from this?" or "What is the lesson here?" When we trust in the journey, knowing that we are growing ourselves through the experiences that come up, we gain perspective that everything will be all right. We begin to see some good in whatever we are experiencing. It's not that we are in denial. Instead, it's a courageous presence that creates a lens of gratefulness for getting through the day-to-day knowing it's all a part of something greater. A knowing that happiness and fulfillment looks different for each of us and we can feel gratefulness for wherever we are now, even if it's messy and imperfect. Since gratitude is the gateway to joy, this mindset leads to greater happiness and fulfillment now. Not when everything is just right. This moment, which is all that we really have. Our life isn't a dress rehearsal, it's now. Let's break it down.

With mindfulness, our three attention skills, inherent in every one of us, are working together. They are concentration power (ability to focus your mind on what you choose), sensory clarity (ability to track and explore your sensory experience as you are experiencing it) and equanimity (allowing your sensory experience to come and go without push or pull). As we become more aware of how we are focusing our attention, our mind becomes more free. It's the ability to pay attention to what's happening in the present moment as it's happening. Too often, we are stuck in anticipating or remembering, instead of being here and now. When we're in the latter mode, we're not able to experience what is happening in the present moment. And this is where we experience joy, love, compassion, curiosity—all the things we need to feel free and happy and be the parent we dreamed we could be for our children.

POSITIVE MINDFULNESS WITH LINDSAY

Positive Mindfulness is combining Attention, Intention, and Self-Compassion to be more aware, courageous, and positive, moment by moment.

1. **Attention:** Three Attention Skills Working Together
   a) *Concentration Power:* The ability to focus your attention on what you choose
   b) *Sensory Clarity:* The ability to track your sensory experience in real time
   c) *Equanimity:* Allowing your sensory experience to come and go without push or pull (Adapted from Shinzen Young, UnifiedMindfulness.com)

2. **Intention:** Having a greater purpose at heart in all that we do. Seeing the good in what is happening with a knowing that it is always there. Trusting that all of our experiences are moving us along on our unique and perfect imperfect path toward greater meaning and fulfillment and happiness.

3. **Self-Compassion:** Choosing to see ourselves and others with kindness and warmth instead of judgment. Trusting love, compassion, joy, and wisdom is our essence and available to us anytime we choose to focus on it. Embracing our imperfections and connecting to others through our shared humanity, knowing we all experience ups and downs and nobody is perfect. And finally, being aware and in this moment instead of lost in a storyline in our head that doesn't serve us and takes away from the joy and peace of being here now. The more we practice these skills, the more they strengthen and we grow, and connect to the essential joy and love within ourselves and others. (Adapted from Dr. Kristen Neff, self-compassion.org)

When we are present we are tapping into the wisdom and intuition that is within us. We are also absorbing the magic of the universe around us. With this attentiveness to what I am experiencing and feeling, I am bringing acceptance to *what is*. I am in a state of non-judgmental acceptance, seeing, hearing, and feeling *what is* going on as it is happening. This means all feelings and emotions (positive and negative) may arise from my thoughts and experiences, but I allow them to come and go. I like to remember Jack Canfield's quote here, "You only have control over three things in your life—the thoughts you think, the images you visualize, and the actions you take (your behavior)." I don't have control over the emotions, situations, and people that come and go. I have control over what I think about them, what I imagine about them and how I react.

We often react with resistance, avoidance, fear, shame, denial, any number of negative responses when things don't go as we hoped or expected them to. We can stay in this negative, resisting place for a while. We begin to attract more of it around us without even realizing that we haven't healed what was inside and it can manifest on the outside until we bring acceptance and compassion into it. It's okay to have these harsh reactions and to feel anger and jealousy and resentment and shame. We are imperfect and will have these negative feelings. Instead of pushing them down and being hard on ourselves for it this is where the positive mindfulness comes in, we give ourselves compassion in these moments. We say to ourselves, "It's okay to feel this way" or "It's natural to be completely overwhelmed and yell at my children." From this compassionate acceptance, we begin to retrain our brain to respond differently when our children trigger us. Through this kindness, comes acceptance, and change. Too often we push these feelings down and quickly judge and criticize ourselves after we react negatively. And this judgment just makes it grow inside us.

We can re-create the storyline that does not serve us (or humanity), one of us as unworthy, unlovable, the bad mother. We are more hurt by the judgment of ourselves than the original act. It leads us to feeling very sad inside and eventually we spread this negative energy into our families. We can give our kids what was handed down to us. Or, we can stop the cycle, by taking a moment to be kind to ourselves and create a new story. We've all done the best we could with the tools we had up until this point. And we are all capable of change. We can start fresh in each moment.

With mindfulness also comes perspective. It is helpful to bring attention to our feelings and emotions and acknowledge them as an outsider looking in. You say, "Wow, a lot of anger is coming up right now. I feel it in my stomach and it's rising through my chest. It's strong." We are choosing to explore our sensory experience with a non-judgmental, awareness. This is creating space between our experience and our response. We can choose a response from a place of acceptance and love. When we practice mindfulness and self-compassion, we can let go of the unmet expectation or whatever it is that is causing hurt in us and embrace *what is*. We can experience happiness without conditions, knowing we are only responsible for our response to what happens to us. We are responsible for the energy we bring to any situation, that part is up to us. Through positive mindfulness and self-compassion, we see some good in whatever we are experiencing knowing whatever is coming up is here to grow some part of us so we may live, love, and serve our families and our world in a more connected and authentic way.

"With mindfulness, we are open to what's actually happening instead of thinking about it. Thought is a picture of reality and sometimes it's off base."

~Lindsay

How do we have positive thoughts about something that feels negative? It takes practice and perspective. Being able to zoom out from our individual experience into the world at large allows us to get unstuck in a negative storyline from difficult emotions. Remembering that there are people who can't have children and are praying to experience what we are experiencing now helps give us perspective. A walk in nature helps our worries seem small in comparison to the bigger picture. Dr. Kristen Neff's research on self-compassion provides the research to back these practices. She describes how our mind's natural tendency is to think, create a sense of self, and look for problems. It's a survival mechanism. It takes creativity to see things differently, yet it is within all of us. There are a lot of different ways we can think. With mindfulness, we are open to what's actually happening instead of thinking about it. Thought is a picture of reality and sometimes it's off base. We all have the capability to think differently and train our brains to think more creatively, positively, and compassionately.

Choosing to think positively about what happens in our life just takes practice. We won't ever get it right all the time, that's what "being human" means. But the more I practice, the more quickly I can recognize when I am stuck in a negative thought pattern. That is a trigger that I am no longer present. I go back to the first step, which is awareness, to bring me back to the present. Then I accept what I am feeling, with compassion for myself. I can tell myself, "It's okay and normal to feel what I feel. We all feel this way at times. We aren't here to be perfect." With self-kindness, I can choose to see some good in it from the perspective of "What am I meant to learn from this?" I can move on, believing I did the best I could and thus evolve into a higher version of myself.

Along with practice, we can begin to activate the more positive creative flow of our mind by practicing meditation or quieting our mind. We know that our mind has two ways of operating. One is the logical, pattern-driven way to see our world and come up with solutions. It's our thinking, physical mind or brain. This creates routines and order, which is needed on some level. But it also creates endless chatter in our heads, telling us what to do and not to do, judging us and others (monkey brain). I feel there is a spiritual mind as well. We feel it when we're fully present, in a flow-state. This is where we let go and feel the pure love that is in us and all around us. It's where creativity, joy, and peace are felt. We're connected in to our deeper purpose, our essence, our soul's mind. As Rumi wrote, "You are not a drop in the ocean. You are the entire ocean in a drop." It's within all of us. Many of us have lost sight of it, spending too much time in our physical mind. It's letting go to what we feel, instead of what we know, and it's always right.

Children operate from this spirited, creative, and joyful place. They are relying on their senses to activate their mind—they haven't learned logic yet. They are using their creativity, imagination, and senses to feel their way through their experiences. This is why they can feel such intense joy and excitement and then frustration and sadness a moment later. We are meant to be present and spirited too, feeling happiness and being open to the experiences and blessings awaiting us. Spending time quieting our mind through a daily meditation practice helps center us, as we tap into our soul's mind, our essence. It helps quiet the part of our mind that operates in only past problems, regrets, and resentments or future worries, fears, and expectations. It also activates the part of our mind that is creatively and openly experiencing the present moment. Many of us have lost connection with our essence, innate creativity, and our inner child wonderment. Taking time to meditate for five minutes, ten minutes, or whatever we can do, helps us reconnect with our oneness. It is harder to parent when we feel disconnected. We need to be open and creative. We should not rely on logic and patterns as parents—especially considering our children's minds do not work that way. The ripple effect of mindfulness is almost palpable. The energetic resonance between Mama and baby or Mama and spouse is almost immediately felt when you are aware.

The Facts

New research demonstrates positive effects mindfulness has on improving our well-being from our health to happiness to resilience and how it spreads to those around us as well, like our children and spouses. One study, as reported on Mindful.org, found that parents who practiced mindful parenting demonstrated less negative emotion and more shared positive emotion with their children, actually reducing some adolescent negative behaviors such as drug use, anxiety, and acting out.[7] Mindfulness helps parents stick to their parenting goals because they aren't getting as caught up in moment-to-moment stressors that can easily trigger them. We want to be well-equipped with the best tools to handle whatever comes up for us emotionally, physically, and mentally—and mindfulness is proving to be one such tool.

While mindfulness helps as children age, the importance of practicing it begins as early as conception. Research shows the mother's state effects a baby even in utero, as the baby is growing his or her own nervous system. There's no question being a parent brings on stress, what we need to do is focus on how to use tools like mindfulness to be more aware, compassionate and accepting, and choose to react purposely, with intention when we feel stressed. And it's never too late to begin practicing positive mindfulness. We all forget and fail and react, but we can begin again fresh each moment. To trust what we feel. Now is a wonderful time to start.

The very practice of mindfulness calls us to accept wherever we are, avoid comparisons and judgment and release feelings of guilt. Each moment we are mindful is a little gift for us and those around us. And the more we do it, the easier and more natural it becomes. It's a process and we are all at different stages of becoming more mindful and self-aware. There's always room for improvement, so let's practice, Mama!

FROM THE FILES OF DR. JESSICA KILLEBREW

Being a new mama is undoubtedly tough, especially for the first-time mother! New mothers not only give birth to their first child, they give birth to their own motherhood. It can be a time filled with doubt, parental guilt, and a fair amount of stress and challenge. It is inevitably a trial and error period (a.k.a. all of motherhood). How we behave and approach mothering is largely determined by how we were mothered. The way we relate to our own little one stems from our very first relationships—for better or for worse.

Mindfulness brings attention to how we are feeling, what we are thinking, and allows us to come from an awakened, less reactive space. We reduce the chance of coming from old patterns and can break free from the stress, anxiety—even depression—often associated with our first run at motherhood. It can bring a sense of feeling grounded, calm, and even peaceful in the moments when we are lost, scared, overwhelmed, and stressed. Being mindful helps us understand how our perception creates reality and gives us a way to work with our internal voice. Mindfulness affects well-being which ultimately allows us to be better mothers. When we are mindful, we can see and experience our children more purely, calmly, and with grounded presence. It helps us wake up, slow down, savor, get intentional. The best part is that it lends us presence so we can really BE with our children. —**Jessica Killebrew, PsyD** (*Meet her on page 108.*)

THE PRACTICE

Now, let's delve into each of these pieces of mindfulness and provide you tools with which to practice. The greatest thing to remember is that *mindfulness is a practice and it's also a process.* We don't become mindful and stay in that state all the time. The goal is to be less reactive and more present and mindful for more moments of the day.

Mindfulness is a Practice

Like anything, mindfulness takes practice. It's like a muscle. The more we work on it, the stronger it becomes and starts working for us. We have to keep practicing it:

1. Quiet the mind through meditation (breathing with intention) or simply sitting in quiet at a set time during the day (maybe in the morning or in the evening). Begin with 2 minutes, then 5 and gradually move up to 10 or more.

2. Practice moment-to-moment walking meditation throughout our daily activities, we can become mindful as we're doing the dishes, sitting in traffic, or on a walk with our baby.

3. Use our breath to bring ourselves back to center at any time during the day. Pausing, focusing on breathing in and out, and remembering that peace begins within us.

It's All About Awareness

Here's why mindfulness is about awareness. When we are aware, we are not lost in our own thoughts. We are not cloudy or in a haze consumed with thoughts about the past, the future, or endless mental chatter that doesn't serve us. We are aware of our surroundings, feelings, and senses. We allow ourselves to really feel this moment and engage in it with all five senses. Let's flip this into a powerful affirmation to jumpstart your mindfulness practice:

I am aware of what I am seeing, hearing, and feeling.
I allow myself to really feel this moment
and engage in it with all of my senses.

The Peaceful Mama's Mindfulness Toolkit

- **Breath:** Use your breath to slow yourself down and bring awareness to the moment by grounding yourself with your body. You can focus on the inward and outward feeling of breath moving through your body and it will calm you and bring you back. Whenever you are feeling overwhelmed, focusing on breath brings you back to a calm state.

- **Labeling (See, Hear, Feel Technique):** Use your senses to simply observe whatever it is you are experiencing in this moment. Call it out to yourself—I'm hearing birds, I'm seeing cars, I'm feeling something in my leg, I'm hearing wind, I'm seeing leaves, I'm feeling my shirt, I'm hearing a train horn. Allow yourself to just feel whatever, openly, without judgment. Do this throughout the day to bring awareness and become present to what you are feeling. This is also helpful when you are stuck on something. This practice can get you away from that thought that is running rampant and into the here and now, the present moment that is peace, neither positive or negative.

- **Self-Compassion.** Compassion is available to all of us and can be transformative. As we become aware of the way we are talking to ourselves with mindfulness, we can choose to see our situation with kindness instead of judgment. We can acknowledge that we feel hurt, whether it was self-imposed or not, it is still hurt. We can put our hand on our heart and give ourselves compassion for what we are feeling; we can say we are not alone in this hurt. We all feel this way from time to time, nothing is perfect all the time. We can then choose to be mindful about what is really happening in the here and now instead of over-identifying and being lost in a storyline in our heads that doesn't serve us now. We must first become present and compassionate with ourselves, then we can extend compassion to others, like our families. Watch your children. Take a few moments to watch your child while she is engaged in an activity or at play. Our children are our Zen masters. They have incredible presence and give their full attention. Just watch and observe them and express gratitude as you observe.

Sidenote: The Beauty of Our Breath

The way to practice being mindful in the midst of our symbiotic connection with our baby is to choose to notice something about ourselves that not even a baby can take away from us: *our breath.* It is our secret wellspring of love, light, energy, and abundance—when we think of it that way. And being aware of it, we are reconnecting to our eternally true self—our Awareness here and now. Compassionately choosing to practice is key. Deciding to BELIEVE this is the source of your well-being—your Breath—gives you what you need to flourish. If you don't breathe, you don't flourish. Gently, creatively, think about when you can make focusing on one or two (or more) breaths a habit. Attaching this practice to habits and tasks of daily living is one very effective tactic.

For example, witness your taking a breath—inhale and exhale—when you first touch your breast or the bottle, holding your hand still on the milk-source. Witness your hand there, witness your breath, where the inhale begins, and when the exhale comes, where you feel it. Curious. Maybe you witness another round of a breath. Then continue doing the next step in the process of being with your baby. You might eventually find you are witnessing yourself experiencing all five-plus senses more vividly as you continue the feeding.

Another task of daily living to use as an anchor for practicing breath-meditation may be urinating—if you're lucky, you get to do it alone! Before or after you eliminate, give your Witnesser self a moment to be mindfully aware of the next breath—inhale and exhale. Creatively create your own plan for practicing. Start small and simple. Being here and now, for one breath, you taste eternity. —**Sheryl Stoller** (*Meet her on page 110.*)

- **3 x 3 x 3 Practice.** In the evenings before you go to sleep, begin a five-minute practice of writing three gratitudes, three worries, and three intentions. You can hand-write it out in a journal or just type it into your phone in a note-taking or journaling app. First jot down a few things you are grateful for from the day. Remember, what we focus on grows. Next, write down a few things that are worrying you or causing you struggle or stress and write them from the lens of asking for guidance. Sometimes getting the worries out of our head and into the universe helps us with coming up with a solution or at least finding peace with it. Finally, write a few intentions for what you hope to accomplish or work on the next day, with the most important thing listed first. Check out PeacefulMamas. com/meditations for an audio version of how to start your 3 x 3 x 3 practice.

- **Perspective.** Getting outside or just thinking about nature, helps you to zoom out and see your experience as rather small in the lens of the larger world around us. You can see how nature just flows and that life can too, if we let it. Look up at the clouds, see the enormity of a tree or the magnificence of the sky, look at an animal or a flower. Everything in nature is perfect and we are too. It's only when we define our experiences as good or bad or less than that everything seems out of alignment. As long as we are experiencing and growing and connecting, we remember that everything is perfectly imperfect and how it is meant to be.

Mindfulness is Being Responsible for Our Thoughts

Mindfulness is noticing our thoughts without judgment, being attentive and aware of them. There will always be people, experiences, feelings and emotions distracting us from feeling love. All we can do is notice these thoughts and feelings that come up, and accept them, and then we have made way for new thoughts that are positive and kind. We can achieve a level of happiness and well-being that is independent of what is happening around us. When we are in a state of observing and noticing, we can bring attention to what is coming up, negative or positive, then can return to the place of love and goodness within each of us. It is who we are, it is what we are, and it is how we are meant to be living.

Mindfulness is a Process

Go easy, Mama. While we aim for more moments of mindfulness every day, remember that there is no ending, no grand finale or Mindfulness Recital. It is an ever-flowing and ongoing process of recognizing when our automatic reactions, disconnection, and discord have taken over and need to be reeled back in. Mindfulness is about creating a kind and respectful relationship with yourself and others and remembering we can start fresh each moment.

THE MINDFUL DAY

I begin each day early, making time for silent meditation. I include a brief period of yogic breathing where I lie on my back with a bolster under my spine at the lung/heart area to deepen my breath and open my heart. Who would think that lying down after lying down all night would be beneficial? It's one of the paradoxes one learns to entertain when practicing mindfulness. After sitting, I enter the day knowing my inner process is alive and kicking, fueling my energy for fulfillment, and turn towards the challenges and delights of the day. Trusting awareness, I use what's called the "backward step" in Zen where, at any moment, I can pause, relax by taking a conscious breath or two, wake up to what's happening right here, right now, and then proceed with what I'm doing. The magic of practicing what's called "the pause," by stopping and taking one or two conscious breaths, is that the breath will always cut through any thought or feeling state temporarily and then we can let go of forcing life to be a certain way (my way) relinquishing what just happened—because it is over. This practice of moving to the freshness in each moment restores my balance and good humor. The more I do it the more quickly the mental stress and physical tension dissolves and I don't carry it with me through the day. It's a practice of restoring oneself to a more peaceful and easeful existence that over time becomes the stable place one lives.

I tend to end the day with what's called "seeing" meditation which involves external and internal reflecting. Seeing meditation is fascinating with its magical opening to what is just outside our external purview. Try it, gaze on something natural, whether it's combined with walking meditation or gazing out a window, or gazing at a natural object—a flower, stone, or whatever you find in the moment. First, find a soft gaze by breathing in and exhaling any tension around the eyes, allowing the eyes to sink back a little into the sockets. As you continue to breathe, allow the in breath to focus on the object in front of you and the out breath to expand your vision peripherally left and right, opening vision more horizontally while keeping a soft gaze. This back and forth movement has the near immediate effect of expanding our physical reality, but just as important, our emotional clinging relaxes and our thoughts release. My internal thinking/reflecting takes the form of curious surprise: "Wow, I had no idea that would happen today and that I would react or respond in that way." It's my way of practicing what's called "beginner's mind." Beginner's mind is realizing that no matter how many hundreds or thousands of times we've done or experienced something, this time, this experience right now has never happened before. For me, it wakes me up to the wonder of my life, the deepest gratitude of my joy, and some calm acceptance of my suffering as well as the suffering and joy of others. —**Margaret Kachadurian, LCSW** (*Meet her on page 109*)

Reflection Time

Like Lindsay, I (Natalie) also practice mindfulness every single day—if you don't practice it already, I hope that by the end of this chapter you will too! It has become an almost addictive habit of mine and it's an addiction I am proud of. I am very conscious of my thoughts and thought patterns, which is extremely helpful when talking about mindfulness because, as Lindsay mentions, awareness is a crucial step in becoming a Peaceful Mama.

Lance and I have recently begun using the phrase "be aware" when Jonah and Skye are bike riding or playing at the park. We decided that saying "be careful" was insinuating that danger was around every bend, whereas "be aware" focused on the importance of staying present in the moment. It's so easy to get caught up in the minutiae of the day and lose sight of the bigger picture. For example, how easy is it to get frustrated with the fact that the dishes are dirty, your back hurts from pregnancy, you're hungry and dinner isn't made yet?! When you are aware of your thoughts, this downward spiral of negativity and complaining focused only on the negative can easily be rectified. When you are aware of your thoughts then you can (somewhat) shift your train of thought. What if instead of complaining about the dishes, your back, and lack of dinner you realize how grateful you are to have so many clothes that you are able to do laundry. How awesome is it to have a washing machine instead of having to clean your clothes by hand? How grateful are you that your back is achy because it is a reminder of the beautiful new life you are creating inside of you and the monumentally amazing task and blessing you have by physically carrying your baby? How sweet is the fact that you have a fridge full of food just waiting to be prepped and eaten?

"If one of your goals of the day is to practice mindfulness and you have remembered to ask yourself a question to bring yourself back to the moment, then you have succeeded. And, of course this becomes a domino effect because the more often you practice something, the more it becomes habitual. Which in turn makes your mindfulness practice habitual and successful."

~ Natalie

With this shift in thinking not only will you start to feel better but you have just experienced mindfulness. You were aware of the rabbit hole of negativity you could go down and you actively changed the trajectory. Go Mama! When we are mindful we are proactive; when we are not, we are reactive. And, those two positions have vastly different outcomes, especially when children are involved.

When I find myself getting impatient and irritable, it is almost always because I am thinking about something else instead of being fully present with my children. Granted, it is nearly impossible to always be in the moment. Our children are gifted this opportunity because they do not have bills to pay, food to buy, and "grown up" responsibilities however, they are always there to remind us of that whenever we have drifted too far off the radar.

Another scenario I find myself in, especially as a new Mama, is when my essential basic needs are not being met. If I am unable to sit down and eat, drink enough water, go to the toilet and properly and thoroughly eliminate, have enough rest, etc., I become irritable and impatient. This can easily spiral out of control if I am not aware of what is happening. Once I notice that this is the reason why I am not behaving the way I truly want to then I can more readily rectify the situation.

As questions for reflection, I'd like to offer the same ones I ask myself when I realize I am not my best self:

- What basic needs are not being met? (i.e., food, water, sleep, bowel and urine elimination)
- Am I thinking/worrying about something in the future?
- Am I worrying about something that is out of my immediate control?
- Is what I am distracted by actually worth my effort, focus and energy right now, or is it something that can wait until another more productive time? For example, do I really need to check Facebook while my son is trying to tell me something, or can the notifications wait until later when I am alone?
- How am I feeling right now? And, is it the emotion that I would like to be feeling?

The answers to these questions will inevitably bring you back to the present moment—activating mindfulness. I find it so interesting how quickly the mind can jump from one thought to another. It's one of the awesome bonuses about being a woman: we can multitask pretty damn well and are super-efficient. It actually amazes me how much Lance has had to work on becoming efficient, when for women I find it is often times effortless and an almost innate quality.

When we are consistently practicing mindfulness, are regularly checking in with ourselves and asking intentional questions, we succeed. Success is personal and it is relative. If one of your goals of the day is to practice mindfulness and you have remembered to ask yourself a question to bring yourself back to the moment, then you have succeeded. And, of course this becomes a domino effect because the more often you practice something, the more it becomes habitual. Which in turn makes your mindfulness practice habitual and successful. The opposite of success is not failure. I'd like to make that clear. I believe everyone is a success, which is why I said it is relative.

It's important to celebrate the wins—big and small, even tiny successes. So, to be crystal clear: everyone is a success, even if they do not remember to practice mindfulness daily. With that being said, when we make a commitment to ourselves and thread mindfulness into our lives, we know it leads to feeling more peaceful and happier with ourselves and our parenting. And, that feels good!

THE EXPERT EXCERPTS

TWO MINDFUL MAMAS: "WHAT WE WISH WE KNEW THEN"

By Jessica Killebrew, PsyD, and Margaret Kachadurian, LCSW

Dr. Jessica: *I had no idea becoming a mother would be so challenging.* Furthermore, that the most challenging aspect would turn out to be myself in the whole mix! Everyone kept telling me that the hardest part would be sleepless nights and inconsolable crying. Yet, it turned out to be less about how to handle the baby and more about me to my surprise. "Wherever you go, there you are," as Confucius was believed to have once said. This couldn't be truer of parenting.

From all the mind chatter to the ever-changing flow of emotions, the common denominator of your experience is you. How you perceive life, interact, and ultimately how you manifest as a parent depends on everything you have become up until this point. Not to mention, your child is drinking you in as they form, create, and unfold from moment-to-moment. It's a crazy-beautiful process that is overwhelmingly profound. Therefore, truly, the most precious nugget of wisdom to raising a healthy little human is to work on yourself. Look deeply, be curious, challenge the perceptions and familial patterns and how they impact the relationship with your child. The best chance they have to fulfill their highest self is for you to become your highest self. It's the biggest and most important thing we can ever do. To be honest, I had no real clue what I was in for or how ripe with growth opportunity being a mother would be!

Jessica Killebrew, PsyD, earned her doctorate in Clinical Psychology with an Integrative emphasis. She specializes in mindfulness-based interventions and currently works with clients in private practice as a coach helping parents and individuals unfold their highest wisdom. She writes, lectures, teaches, mentors, facilitates workshops and conferences and loves generating community surrounding her passion for conscious parenting and mindful living. Dr. Killebrew is a "mindful mama" to two most curious little ones and believes in the power of slowing down, sinking in and savoring.

Margaret: *I would have trusted myself more and noticed more quickly when I got caught in harsh self-criticism.* I would have developed the skills of mindfulness to both notice and then let go of my desired outcome, opening to more possibilities. This would have released me from so many years of attending "The School of Hard Knocks." I've learned there is a "School of Soft Knocks" and I with mindfulness go there more often! The magic available to mothers is realizing our children are Zen masters because they live in the moment playing with life and so can teach us by asking us to enter that moment with them. Getting down on the floor with them and observing their play, holding and rocking them in our laps, singing to them, touching their fingers and toes, face and body—such simple yet profoundly perfect moments of interconnecting are to be had now—not later when the dishes are done. Tasks are endless and people come first is still my learning. Play is essential and just as essential is a ready sense of humor. Babies and children are always ready for both and can give us countless moments of delight if we're willing to be sparked by them.

Margaret Kachadurian, LCSW, is a licensed clinical social worker who specializes in teaching meditation and mindfulness-based stress reduction (MBSR) programs. As a social worker, with advanced training through the Center for Mindfulness in Worcester, MA, she has taught MBSR to people in community settings including parent groups to develop coping and resiliency skills, cancer wellness groups, and mental health professionals working in violence-prevention including those vulnerable to poverty and mental illness. She is dedicated to offering mindfulness training—the simple, yet, powerful capacity to be awake, aware and actively attentive to ones' self, others and life situations—as skills of well-being that can be learned.

A Mother's Meditation on Mindfulness

By Sheryl Stoller

Mindfulness means I am *practicing* actually being in my life while it is happening, living it, and not missing the here and now. Consciously choosing what I am giving my full-on presence, energy, and time to—and how—is my being mindful. It means noticing what all parts of me need, and being gentle with myself when wounds and pains from my past, fears about the future, thoughts, or feelings try to decide for me.

When I am mindful of the dynamics inside of me, I can give myself what I need earlier. Being the Awareness, self AS Awareness, being the Witnesser, I know the earliest bodily sensations in me that indicate I am triggered. And when I mindfully notice that in my body, I can mindfully, without drama (at least less of it), use it as my cue to turn towards myself with curiosity and compassion: *What are you trying to tell me, sweetie?* I get to use the information provided by this incredible system—my body, my mind, my spirit—and integrate it all, for discerning what the moment is calling for from me for the well-being of all…the well-being of my own *inner* child and of the actual baby in front of me.

Being mindful, I notice the abundance that both surrounds and is in me, whatever chaos and adversity is presenting itself. My mind is full—aware of my mind, body, soul, and the whole of me—aware that I have me, in each breath, I can access what I need—from me.

When I am mindful, I give myself a precious gift: I access myself as my own compassionate, capable Ally. I become heart-centered towards myself and my child. Our being mindful to be heart-centered is the most precious and critically important place to be for effectively enabling our children, ourselves, and our relationships to flourish—now and forever.

Sheryl Stoller is a PCI Certified Parent Coach® at both Stoller Parent Coaching and The Center for Identity Potential, a regular guest speaker for organizations, and the mother of three intense, gifted/twice-exceptional children who are now flourishing young adults. Sheryl draws on her professional and personal experience as she specializes in coaching parents privately and in groups, in person and online, equipping parents to consciously create the emotional-legacy™ they intend. She offers a twice-monthly group for "Nurturing Consistency in Getting A Compassionate Hold of Yourself"™ in Oak Park, Illinois, which is soon to be available online.

The Wrap-Up on Mindfulness

Of the many gifts of mindfulness practice, its greatest may be how we can choose to feel positive about a present situation that seems negative. We can choose the affirmation: *I trust in a greater whole.* This zoom-out helps us see our life as just one piece of a larger puzzle that doesn't revolve around us. With this, we can trust that we are not meant to like every experience in life but instead *grow through it* into a more conscious, whole version of our self able to fulfill our purpose here. This trust helps us realize that others too are growing through their own experiences. We can then experience the last piece of mindfulness, which is gratitude for our experience, whatever it was, because of how we grew through it. And gratitude is the gateway to joy.

"Each moment affords us a new opportunity to work with some degree
of kindness with our own automaticity, fears, and expectations and
the very real effects they can have, and learn from them."

—Myla and Jon Kabat-Zinn
Everyday Blessings: The Inner Work of Mindful Parenting

The Fourth MAM_AHH Moment
ABUNDANCE

Abundance is all about perspective. Look around—we can choose lack or abundance every day. Our children represent an abundance of love. In nature, there is an abundance of beauty. And, in any situation, we can show and feel an abundance of gratitude. Begin blessing everything in life with feelings of genuine gratitude for what we have. Because when we *feel* grateful, life changes.

We encourage you to include writing "gratitudes" in your daily practice. Set aside a consistent time of the day to sit down and write what you are thankful for that particular day or moment. Writing gratitudes before falling asleep at night or first thing in the morning is a powerful way to harness the energy of abundance. Perhaps it's a ritual that you do every time you put your baby into the crib. You can keep a pen and notebook next to your bed and implement that practice into your routine. Or maybe, you keep your phone handy and have a little page in a note-taking app called Gratitudes and type a quick gratitude in after the baby has fallen asleep on you. Perhaps it's just the act of turning moments into magic by recognizing the beauty in being present with yourself, your baby, your partner and/or other supportive souls who are there for you.

Gratitude is more than saying thank you. It is more than being polite or recognizing lovely things around you. Genuine gratitude is a loving appreciation of the sounds, smells, feelings, emotions, touch and taste of life. It is when your heart sings, your body smiles and your soul feels sunshine and flowers. It takes time, consistency, dedication and joy to cultivate a heart full of gratitude. And, you deserve to feel that way. Remember, it is your choice. Start small.

Before eating a meal, you can simply say a gratitude prayer for the food:

> *Thank you for the food before me.*
> *Allow it to nourish every cell in my body with vibrant health,*
> *enrich my mind and soul,*
> *And always remind me of how grateful I am.*

Ask yourself—what does the word "wealth" mean to you? Our automatic response tends to define wealth as having lots of money. However, wealth can also be thought of as abundance, prosperity, and generosity.

In contrast, the opposite of abundance is lack. Are you lacking in any of these areas: confidence, relationships, satisfaction, serenity, and/or deep fulfillment?

We are only able to genuinely give when we ourselves have been properly nourished. As loving and conscious wives, Mamas and Mamas-to-be, sisters and friends, we MUST meet our fundamental needs. It is imperative and it is a requirement.

It's as simple as putting the oxygen mask on yourself first before helping anyone else. As women, we have a tendency to put everyone else's needs above our own. And if we do take a few moments, hours, days to ourselves, we may feel guilty or like we are not doing our "job." I call bullshit (again).

We owe it to ourselves, our sisterhood and all of humanity to take back motherhood and womanhood! When our needs, wants and desires are being met, we are able to lovingly and purposely give back to those in our lives—family, friends, community, etc. Abundance practice is a form of preventative medicine. We don't want to get to a point where we are completely depleted and have diminished our own basic and fundamental priorities. There can be balance and harmony in our life and in our family—and it is intimately tied to our abundant consciousness and our attitude of gratitude.

The Facts

In five very specific studies on implementing intentional acts of gratitude into the lives of people who were experiencing various symptoms/illnesses, participants' well-beings improved. It was not only noticeable to the participants, but studies confirmed these results with diagnostic testing. Simple tasks such as keeping a gratitude journal enabled participants to report fewer physical symptoms, less physical pain, increased sleep and improved quality of sleep. Additionally, incorporating consistent gratitude practices showed a significant decrease in systolic blood pressure, as well as less stress and more happiness. The benefits are pretty impressive and the task at hand is relatively simple. It's just a matter of reminding yourself to practice these moments of gratitude until they become habitual.[8-12]

The Practice

Abundance can carry us through all of the other MAMAHH practices because it has to do with mindset. As we begin practicing MAMAHH, we start to feel the positive effects of it in all areas of our life, not just parenting. This is because it starts with our mindset, which touches our everything. It matters what we believe about where we are now, where we want to be, and where we feel we *deserve* to be, and how we are going to get there. Life happens and it can happen to us or with us. Our own mindset is the only thing we can control. That is a choice we make. All of the MAMAHH practices allow life to move with us and as we start to practice, we will start living abundantly. We attract blessings when we are living and acting in a positive way, treating ourselves and others well, thinking positively about where we are, and excitedly envisioning where we want to be.

- **It all starts with acceptance.** We must first accept our current situation and then become truly honest with ourselves, our intentions, and our goals. That is our truth. When we are not truthful and accepting of our own selves, then we cannot expect the abundant life blessings to just appear. We must put in the work. Wherever we are *is* perfect. Even if it does not feel like perfection. We must choose to trust that it is perfect because it is exactly what got us here today. And that is perfect. It is only when we compare ourselves to others that we begin to question ourselves and our status. When we can truly accept where we are, then we can move forward positively. With acceptance of where we are now, we can also find a place of appreciation within us. With appreciation of what we have, we feel gratitude. An appreciative, gracious mindset brings about more things for which to be grateful. It's a simple Law of Attraction yet it seems hard for many of us to think this way. Everything around us tells us to think differently. Once we accept and appreciate, we can start to think about what we want in our life. We can and should dream big. We deserve to live a life of abundance. By focusing our attention on what we really want, we are bringing forth the experiences to make it happen. Opportunities arise, people show up, and life happens before us once we start believing and trusting and letting go.

- **Bless abundance in others.** It's easy to think negatively about others' good fortune, but that only creates more negativity and feelings of lack within us. There are abundant blessings for all of us. It is limitless. Don't let another person's good fortune feel like that makes less for you. Bless others and trust in life bringing it to you as well.

- **Set positive boundaries.** Start to look at the people, experiences, and activities in your life and whether they bring you up or down. Say "no" to the things that don't raise you up. We stopped watching the news, completely. Like, we never watch the news. It is simply not on in our houses and life is so much better. I'll catch news on my phone here and there. But on my phone, I can control the news outlets I want to hear from. They are positive. The media has become so negative, it's mostly about spreading drama and negativity. Remember, saying "no" to something means you are saying "yes" to something better—something better for yourself, and for your family.

- **Speak positively.** Really look at your language and the words you choose to use. It's easy to say "I can't." If you must, then change it to "I am not able to yet." Change "if" statements to "when." Starting a gratitude practice really helps with this. Writing out what you are grateful for and what you hope or pray for every evening (for example) is a tremendous practice to start. It plants the seed in your mind and soon you will start realizing the positive thoughts within your head and heart.

- **Remember your children, remember yourself.** You know all the good wishes you have for your children? Try some of those out on yourself! Our children pick up on what we feel inside. They learn how to see the world by how we view the world. Our mindset makes all the difference. We have to choose to be positive and trust that life is happening to help us grow and flourish into who we are meant to be here, someone with a great purpose. We have to live with a trust, knowing abundance is our birthright.

- **Be clear on your desires. Ask for it.** This is where both visualization and journaling really help. We have to be clear about where we are going and what we want in life. That is how we start abundantly receiving all that life is ready to give us. We have to be ready for it.

Reflection Time

The practice of abundance begins with taking a simple inventory: What kind of self-care and self-love practices and daily gratitudes are you already doing? What can you implement to take your practice to the next level? And, what times throughout your day can you realistically begin implementing this practice so it becomes like second nature?

Write it down, affirm it and then take notes—see what gratitudes are already alive in you and find new ones inspired by this list of questions for reflection.

- **Will You Wake Up in a State of Gratitude?** As previously mentioned in the book, the beginning and the end of the day may be two times where rituals and habits can easily be formed. Imagine if when you wake up every morning your first thoughts are of gratitude and love. Before you place your feet on the floor to get out of bed, you've set your positive intention for the day. It could be something as simple as "Love is patient, love is kind. I am patient, I am kind. I am love." How good would that feel?

- **Will You Combine Abundant Mindset with Hygiene?** You always (hopefully) brush your teeth, so why not add a little self-care into your morning routine? Roll your foot on a massager or tennis ball as you are brushing your teeth to loosen up the muscles in your feet and get the blood circulating throughout your body, and give thanks for your amazing temple. In the shower as your soap your body, thank your legs and feet for being strong and powerful, and for taking you from place to place with beauty, strength, grace and ease.

- **Will You Look at Your Body in the Mirror and Thank It?** Thank your beautiful womanly body and Mama parts for sexual pleasure, creating and birthing life, for connecting you to hundreds of millions of women around the world.

  - Thank your breasts for their incredible ability to connect to your divine femininity.
  - Thank your arms for hugging and holding and providing comfort, love and peace to yourself, your family, your friends.
  - Thank your spine for being so strong and so flexible that it is able to hold and support your body in daily activities.
  - Thank your neck and throat for connecting your brain to your body, for being the channel and the pathway to mental and physical peace.
  - Thank your mouth for the ability to communicate and speak your mind, show your love and embrace your personal power through words. And, also for kissing.
  - Thank your nose for the blessed ability to smell the morning dew on the flowers in your garden, or the salty ocean air at the beach.
  - Thank your eyes for the miracle of sight witnessing the beauty all around you.
  - Thank your eyelashes for being thick, full, curly and a protective barrier for your eyes. (This is a new body part I, Natalie, have become grateful for since I nearly lost them in a sketchy eyelash extension application.)

- **Will You Breathe in Gratitude?** Throughout the day remind yourself to breathe, deeply, fully and consciously. Set a few alarms on your phone if you need a reminder. Mindful breathing brings you back to the present and enables you to stay connected to the present moment, the only place where you can—you guessed it—experience gratitude and abundance consciousness.

- **Will You Scribe a Few Words of Thanks Before You Sleep?** As you close your eyes at night, take a few minutes to remember three things you said or did that made you proud that day. Thank yourself for having a connection to the divine and for following your intuition. Thank yourself for anything else that resonates with you. Be genuine. Be authentic. Be you.

THE EXPERT EXCERPTS
ABUNDANCE MINDSET FOR MAMAS

By Michelle Brown

How to weave abundance into daily life while raising a new bundle of joy? A great question that I finally figured out with my third baby! On those long nights that fade into dawn during the newborn stage, I began to play in my head all of the things I was grateful for. Instead of focusing on my exhaustion I would thank my sweet baby for allowing me to breastfeed her. Or when I began to bottle feed her, I would thank her for this time to bond. I would see the sun come up and give thanks that I get to start my day with my little girl snuggled close.

The co-author of this book, Natalie, inspired me to wake up ready to work and to utilize the wee early hours of the day after feeding the baby. This led me to being able to expand my business in a huge way with a newborn! Getting around fellow moms with an abundance mindset is huge! And fortunately that's what my business is focused on. I truly believe abundance is a mindset that moms must commit to seeking out and internalizing. Choose abundance. Choose positivity.

What you resist persists. So don't resist or push away from the demand of a newborn. Embrace them and find the beauty in the moments. When I made up my mind to focus on being thankful, I had the easiest, most beautiful fourth trimester. AND my husband and I asked ourselves two questions on those long nights…did we change the baby, and did the baby get enough milk? If so we knew we had done everything we could and that the baby just needed swaddles and snuggles! In my work, I want to make sure to transmit the mindset insight of not just surviving a newborn but thriving AND the practical solution of feeding and nurturing our baby in that new baby stage.

Michelle Brown, Founder and CEO of the iHelpMoms website, is a mom on a mission to connect fellow moms to the top resources to make motherhood easier. As a mom of three kids under five, Michelle knows firsthand the importance of having a support system to balance work, motherhood and fulfillment. iHelpMoms brings together the top doctors, dentists, Mommy and Me, lactation consultants, doulas, baby nurses, midwives and more—connecting moms to the resources they need to experience a beautiful birth and a peaceful transition into life with a baby. Michelle is dedicated to giving moms access to excellent family providers, prosperity and peace along the journey of motherhood.

The Priorities of an Abundant Mama

By Tonya Rineer

I wish I had known (and actually believed) that it was OK to ask for help. The littlest things can make such a HUGE difference: having someone prepare a Crockpot meal, getting a sitter so you can take a nap or get a pedicure, or delegating some of the household chores. When you're so busy doing your "job" (which by the way is a 24-7 gig with no days off) it's hard to make time for yourself. But by asking for help so you can take care of YOU, you are doing a few things:

> *"Give yourself grace and every day, look in the mirror and tell yourself, 'You're an amazing mom and you're doing a great job!' ... Give yourself permission to toot your own horn ... YOU deserve it!!!"*
>
> *~ Tonya*

1. Raising your vibe (and your "point of attraction" in the Law of Attraction teachings), 2. Practicing abundance, 3. Replenishing the energy it takes to be a great mom, and 4. Setting an example for those around you (especially your kids) by teaching them how important it is to take time for yourself!

You have just taken on the hardest job in the world! There is no training program. No manual. No rules to go by. You get to make the rules. Give yourself grace and every day, look in the mirror and tell yourself, "You're an amazing mom and you're doing a great job!" We remember all of our baby's milestones—her first steps, the first time she sleeps through the night, the first tooth—but are you remembering to celebrate yours? YOU are the one behind these magical moments. YOU are the one maintaining your sanity and keeping it together on two hours' sleep. YOU are the one who intuitively understands all of her cries and knows how to soothe her. YOU are the one who can balance her in one arm, talk on the phone and still manage to get dinner on the table. YOU are incredible and YOU deserve to be celebrated! Don't wait for someone else to take notice of all the wonderful things you're doing. Give yourself permission to toot your own horn and celebrate the incredible journey you're on. YOU deserve it!!!

Tonya Rineer is a wife, mother and innovative Money Mindset Coach who knows firsthand how female entrepreneurs can struggle to determine their value. Through the Profit Party, she seeks to revolutionize the way women think and feel about money and business. Her action-oriented style offers actionable tools to help women control their finances, transform their beliefs about money and dramatically increase their profit potential.

ABUNDANCE IS ... ABUNDANT!

By Velvet Chong, RN

Abundance fills the air and we must only be present and accept this to receive it. Events or circumstances happen in our lives and we can lose sight of this hope, of this abundant energy of love filling our every breath. Observing children is an easy way to regain hope as they are bubbling with abundance. When we were financially struggling and it was difficult to see this hope, I was guided to relisten to Deepak Chopra's *Seven Spiritual Laws of Success*. He reminded me of how the law of attraction works (I've heard it for years but we all need reminders throughout this journey) and if I wanted to receive, I needed to give. My daughter sparked an idea and we practiced giving daily while living in gratitude of what we had and more employment opportunities arose for me. There is help and support our there in the universe. You just have to seek it.

When there is lack of sleep, showers, and hot meals due to the care of your little miracle, it is easy to fall into that lower frequency where negative thoughts repeat and feelings of overwhelm, overstress and undernourishment arise. With phone apps and online groups, you can find your tribe of support in local or distant moms who are in your very shoes and have ideas to boost you up. There are beautiful moments outside on those rainy days. Breathe in and center yourself during your nursing or feeding sessions and know there is an abundance of love waiting for you.

Breathe in again and open yourself up to receive it.

Being in nature is another great way to observe and receive abundant joy and love. Take a stroll at least once daily to engage the senses and be present in this miraculous space. You may find tiny flowers emerging from a crack in the sidewalk or little leaves in the shape of hearts to remind you of the abundance in the air. It is so important for us moms to stay in balance and model this balance for our children, to show them this abundance and this hope in these times.

Velvet Chong, RN and Healing Touch Practitioner, is a health and wellness practitioner serving all ages with energy medicine. She combines her knowledge of studies in Ayurvedic healing, Naturopathy, Whole Food healing and Energy Medicine, including Homeopathy, Quantum Touch, Essential Oil Aromatherapy and Qi Gong to activate the body's innate self-healing abilities toward balanced expressions of health and conscious living. She is the owner of The Velvet Lotus, a wife, and a mother of two.

The Wrap-Up on Abundance

So, Mama, how will you practice abundance when it doesn't always seem like there's an abundance of time? What if you only have five minutes? By now, we hope it's sounding pretty simple, once you get into the habit of being grateful and practicing MAMAHH. It's all about being aware of your thoughts. For example, as soon as you are about to get upset about sitting in traffic, you can interrupt that thought by being grateful that you have a car to drive you places. Or when you have laundry piled high and are none too pleased to delve into it. I often think about how grateful I am to have an abundant amount of clothes for my family and me. Or, turn on your favorite podcast and listen while you fold. It may soon become an activity you look forward to. Or when I am able to sit in quiet and take a deep, intentional breath. I am grateful for the opportunity (even if it is just a thirty seconds) to actually focus on my breath and give gratitude for my lungs and respiratory systems functioning with grace and ease. Being grateful begins the moment you open your eyes, and it can easily be threaded throughout your day. Again, we meet our sweet friend, gratitude. Abundance, and all the good things in life, always comes back to it!

Abundance Classics: Recommended Reading List

Here are just a few books we consider "abundance classics" that deserve space in a Peaceful Mama's library...

The Secret
by Rhonda Byrne

Wishes Fulfilled: Mastering the Art of Manifesting
by Dr. Wayne Dyer

Ask and It is Given: Learning to Manifest Your Desires
by Esther and Jerry Hicks

Thick and Grow Rich
by Napoleon Hill

The Wisdom of Florence Scovell Shinn: Four Complete Books
by Florence Scovell Shinn

This is by no means an exhaustive selection! As we discover amazing new books, we curate an updated list at www.PeacefulMamas.com.

HEALTH

Health is holistic. It is about mind, body, and spirit. Its definition is unique and individual. No diagnostic test in the world can assess an individual's total picture of health. Health is about providing the body with proper nutrients, hydration, exercise, and self-care, thus satisfying the multidimensional needs that we all deserve to have fulfilled. We believe taking care of our health is the most important factor in being a Mama.

Finding your optimal health will enhance your life in countless ways. Remember, healthy doesn't necessarily mean skinny, although losing weight does tend to be a positive side effect to eating clean, whole foods. But, health is not solely about food, it is about nourishing your body, mind, and spirit. Physical health, emotional health, spiritual health, social health and mental health all play a part in our overall well-being. They are equally important in obtaining homeostasis. If one area is lacking, your whole system can be thrown off balance.

This section has an intense focus on how YOU, the Mama, can make actionable changes in your everyday life to be healthier, decrease stress, and BE happier.

THE FACTS

First, let's get clear on what health is and what it is not: **Health is** attainable, especially when we implement a gradual accumulation of little efforts, a.k.a. practicing MAMAHH Moments. Health encompasses food, exercise, home environment, relationships, spirituality, joy, creativity, finances, career, education, social life and so much more.

Health is NOT the absence of dis-ease. Health is not "going on a diet." There's a reason "diet" has the word die in it—you are setting yourself up for failure. Switch your view to "lifestyle change" and prepare for success.

The opposite of health is dis-ease. Crucial times to find homeostasis in our body is pre-conception, pre-natal and again postpartum as our bodies heal.

Since we have already discussed Movement, this Health chapter is dedicated to other areas of health. Here we will slim down (pun intended) our selection of facts about health into four categories: **Water, Sleep, Inflammation/Stress,** and **Food.**

Like a marriage, each category must work cohesively with and complement the other in order to create and maintain balance—and in this sense, we want you to become a health detective. If you focus solely on exercise or solely on diet, your health will not be optimal, as your body and mind will be imbalanced. Think about a garden. If you water your garden over and over again but offer it no sunshine and no fresh soil and no love, your garden won't thrive. If you exercise over and over again but eat foods that don't nourish you, allow negative self-talk and breathe in toxins all day, you should not expect optimal health. Healthy people focus on all the facets that make-up health, instead of obsessing over just one or two.

WATER

Water plays a crucial role in a variety of body functions. It helps nutrients reach cells, aids in digestion, removes toxins from your body, even regulates your body temperature—water is not only necessary but vital! Staying hydrated is super important while your precious baby is growing inside of you. Most often we hear that eight cups of water a day is sufficient but it's often too low. Many dietitians and nutritionists recommend following this equation: your current weight divided by 2 equals how many ounces of water you should drink. For example, if you weigh 100 pounds (for easy math) divided by 2 = 50 ounces of water per day. *Keep in mind that number is for women who are neither pregnant nor nursing.* So, you will absolutely require more water than you might initially suspect! Additionally, your diet (what foods you are eating) will also play a role in your hydration levels. If you are drinking broth, soups, herbal teas, juicy fruits, green juices, etc., your individual water requirements may vary. Dehydration and preterm labor are serious issues that can arise when we are not aware of our bodies and babies' needs. Oftentimes, pregnant Mamas, especially Mamas who already have one or more babies at home, can become distracted with the day to day and drinking enough water seems to take a back burner to everyone and everything else. Keep in mind that if you are nauseated and experiencing "morning" sickness, you may be losing water. And, if that's the case it's even more important to stay hydrated. Sometimes plain water can be unappealing; perhaps adding some lemon juice or lime juice will help you drink a little extra. Coconut water is also a great addition not only because of the amazing electrolyte content but also because it is high in potassium, which is another crucial vitamin necessary for you and your baby. For more detailed information and statistical facts, please check out this article summarizing the insight of Dr. Joel Fuhrman, MD: babble.com/pregnancy/water-and-pregnancy/ and facts noted from Kellymom.com, a wonderful website dedicated to pregnant and nursing Mamas.

SLEEP

Although a simple concept, sometimes sleep is not an easy feat—especially if you are in the later stages of pregnancy and are physically uncomfortable, or already have children in the house. Yet, it is still an important component of overall health. One of the interesting facts about sleep is that not all sleep is created equal. For example, if you are a night owl and tend to fall asleep after midnight, you may not be getting the most rejuvenating sleep you could get if you went to bed before 10 p.m. Even if you sleep an extra couple hours in the morning to "make up" for the night before it may not be restorative. It's not always about the quantity of sleep, but instead the quality that really makes a difference. For detailed information about sleep and its effects check out the *TIME* magazine article by Markham Heid, "What's the Best Time to Sleep?" at www.time.com/3183183/best-time-to-sleep/.

Also, keep in mind that, as we have mentioned several times throughout the book, we are all unique individuals. There are plenty of people who can get six hours of sleep a night and are perfectly capable of performing at their peak the next day, while other people seem to require more zzz's to function optimally. And, of course, when you are performing the Herculean task of baby growing you will need more sleep. Every day and every phase of our lives will be different, as will our sleep.

According to Valley Sleep Center: "Our circadian rhythm uses light and the absence of light as triggers to help our body determine where we are in the 24-hour cycle of our day. When it gets dark, melatonin is released and we get tired and go to sleep. When the sun comes up, the light triggers a biological response that wakes us up. Light therapy mimics this pattern and exposes you to bright lights for a specified amount of time upon waking. Over several weeks this can help adjust your waking time to be earlier in the morning."[13]

Avoiding products that contain caffeine is a good idea, as caffeine can affect your sleep pattern and circadian rhythm, not to mention it increases your urine output, thus leading to dehydration, a definite no-no. Speaking of harmonizing with natural cycles, you can also take control of your health by syncing up your menstrual cycle with the moon, aligning your circadian rhythm, and becoming more self-aware of how your body ebbs and flows. Check out the book *Lunaception: A Feminine Odyssey into Fertility and Contraception* by Louise Lacey.

INFLAMMATION/STRESS

There are many things that can cause inflammation, stress, and/or dis-ease in the body. Each of these can impact the health and wellness of you and baby. It can also affect the likelihood of conceiving, maintaining a healthy pregnancy, and healing postpartum. Identifying and managing these issues are key in optimizing your health. You want your reproductive system, lymphatic system, digestive system and all the other "systems" to work harmoniously together in a pain-free, disease-free body.

Our physical body processes emotions just as we would mentally and emotionally. Remember the section where we talked about inflammation being the body's way of showing us it is angry? My closest friends and family know that my go-to response to dis-ease is to remove gluten. We giggle about it, I try not to preach about it, but the facts are clear: gluten, dairy, sugar, caffeine, soy, and GMOs are all inflammation-causing foods. When your body is under attack by inflammation, my first suggestion would be to eliminate these culprits.

When we are under physical stress, we get sore or achy. When we are constantly having negative self-talk, we can become depressed or mentally exhausted. And, when someone has screamed at us we feel emotionally bruised. A physical bruise will show up black and blue, a twisted ankle will be swollen and red, and a cut on your arm will bleed. These are all reactions we can see with our eyes and feel in our bodies. We see it and feel it, therefore we believe that it is there.

In contrast, with depression, mental exhaustion, Alzheimer's, etc., we cannot see it or feel it (unless of course we get an MRI, PET or CAT scan). Since we lose the visual with these symptoms, an outsider may not know you are suffering. And, of course, when we are emotionally bruised, it is something very personal and private that only we ourselves know and feel.

However, the common denominator in all of these scenarios is inflammation. When I hear the word "inflammation," I think red, swollen, sensitive and ANGRY! We may not think of our bodies as having emotions like anger, but in Traditional Chinese Medicine, specific emotions are linked to our organs. For example: anger is associated with the liver and fear with the kidneys. So, if you are having difficulty controlling your anger, it is quite possible your liver needs a good detox. And, if you find yourself constantly living in fear, you may need to tonify your kidneys. The liver, kidney and colon are three of our biggest detox pathways and when these are blocked, dis-ease occurs as we open ourselves up to a host of problems, physical, mental, emotional.

Inflammation is nothing more than the body's reaction to a stressor—food, environment, chemical, emotional, physical, etc. Any diagnosis ending in "itis" indicates inflammation is present. Colitis, appendicitis, tendinitis, sinusitis, arthritis, bronchitis. Colitis is inflammation of the colon. Appendicitis is inflammation in your appendix…you get the picture.

The question is often, "What can I do to relieve the inflammation?" as opposed to "What can I do to stop the CAUSE of the inflammation?" Once the body is not under attack, then we can narrow down the cause, instead of putting a Band-Aid on the symptom. The latter looks like taking Tylenol for a cold versus boosting the immune system with extra vitamin C, zinc, echinacea, etc. One suppresses the immune system while the other supports the immune system and allows the body to use its innate wisdom to activate the body's own medicine and self-healing mechanism.

Begin paying attention to how your body functions whenever you eat certain foods, drink various beverages, breathe in different smells, hear particular sounds, and see certain images. As a result of our internal and external environments, as well as our family health history, culture, and background, each of us will handle "stress" differently. That stress comes in the form of food, drink, people, thoughts, and our environment.

Some people are naturally better detoxifiers and can withstand more exposure to stress and toxins before they have symptoms. Others need more support. Learning as much as you can about the products you use, the buildings you live in, and the water you drink is crucial to preventing or fighting inflammation.

You do not have to live with pain or discomfort. Your body is smart, you just need to learn how to listen to it.

FOOD

Health is also about making the right food choices, and in this department, Knowledge is Power. Keep in mind the importance of bio-individuality—know that your perfect diet is designed especially for you. The nutritional requirements for preconception, prenatal and postpartum women vary. Please keep that in mind as you are reading through these sections. We recommend *Yeah Baby!* by Jillian Michaels for a detailed breakdown of foods for prenatal women.

There is so much conflicting dieting advice today that it is nearly impossible not to be confused. And it seems the more research you do, the more confused you become. We take a highly comprehensive approach to health because it is not solely about food, but should be viewed holistically. One person's food is another person's poison. We are all unique and have bio-individuality and therefore require different things to function optimally. One of the goals is to figure out how YOUR body is designed to thrive. And, the best way to do that is to experiment on yourself.

In planning for pregnancy and postpartum, we are aware that excess weight is unwanted, unnecessary and in some cases unhelpful. When you follow these principles of health, weight loss is a side effect, but remind yourself that optimal health is the goal. Of course you can use a scale as a tool, but the best way to measure weight loss is by your clothes. It's most important to feel healthy in your own body. A healthy body is more than a mirror or scale can show you. Feeling healthy is significantly more important than looking healthy, which tends to be clouded by an inaccurate depiction of societal ideals. With that being said, if you are a breastfeeding Mama, please remember that your nutritional needs are also slightly different than if you bottle feed. Helping to strengthen your baby developmentally, immunologically, and nutritionally through your milk is of vital importance and should be viewed as such.

According to the U.S. National Library of Medicine:

"For most normal-weight pregnant women, the right number of calories is:

About 1,800 calories per day during the first trimester.

About 2,200 calories per day during the second trimester.

About 2,400 calories per day during the third trimester."[14]

Food is many things: it's tradition, culture, comfort, love, fuel, and most importantly—when we eat nutrient-dense foods—it is nutrition.

One of the biggest misconceptions we have as consumers is the idea that fat is bad and low calorie is good. The advertising industry has done an impeccable job in convincing the public that fake foods, genetically modified foods, chemical and laboratory foods are nutritious, acceptable foods for our families. This couldn't be further from the truth. What you want to look for are ingredients you can pronounce, preferably ingredients that are real foods, not with numbers or words that sound like they belong in a chemistry book. Here are some ingredients to avoid and the reasons why they are harmful:

- **Artificial Colors:** Chemical compounds made from coal-tar derivatives to enhance color (linked to allergic reactions, fatigue, asthma, skin rashes, hyperactivity and headaches)
- **Artificial Flavorings:** Cheap chemical mixtures that mimic natural flavors (linked to allergic reactions, dermatitis, eczema, hyperactivity, and asthma; can affect enzymes, RNA and thyroid)
- **Artificial Sweeteners:** Highly-processed, chemically-derived, zero-calorie sweeteners found in diet foods and name-brand products to reduce calories per serving (look for Acesulfame-K and Aspartame on the ingredient label; can negatively impact metabolism; some have been linked to cancer, headaches, dizziness and hallucinations)
- **Butylated hydroxytoluene (BHT), Butylated hydroxyanisole (BHA), Tertiary butylhydroquinone (TBHQ):** Compounds that preserve fats and prevent them from becoming rancid (may result in hyperactivity, asthma, rhinitis, dermatitis, tumors and skin issues; can affect estrogen balance and levels)
- **Brominated Vegetable Oil (BVO):** Chemical that boosts flavor in many citric-based fruit and soft drinks (increases triglycerides and cholesterol; can damage liver, testicles, thyroid, heart and kidneys)
- **High Fructose Corn Syrup (HFCS):** Cheap alternative to cane and beet sugar that sustains freshness in baked goods and blends easily in beverages to maintain sweetness (may predispose the body to turn fructose into fat; increases risk for type-2 diabetes, coronary heart disease, stroke and cancer; isn't easily metabolized by the liver)
- **Monosodium Glutamate (MSG):** Flavor enhancer in restaurant food, salad dressing, chips, frozen entrees, soups and more (may stimulate appetite and cause headaches, nausea, weakness, wheezing, edema, change in heart rate, burning sensations and difficulty in breathing)
- **Olestra:** An indigestible fat substitute, used primarily in foods that are fried and baked, that inhibits absorption of some nutrients (linked to gastrointestinal disease, diarrhea, gas, cramps, bleeding and incontinence)

- **Shortening, Hydrogenated and Partially Hydrogenated Oils (Palm, Soybean and others):** Industrially created fats used in more than 40,000 food products in the U.S. as they are cheaper than most other oils (contain high levels of trans fats, which raise bad cholesterol and lower good cholesterol, contributing to risk of heart disease)
- **Sodium Nitrite and Nitrate:** Preserves, colors and flavors cured meats and fish and prevents botulism (but can combine with chemicals in stomach to form nitrosamine—a carcinogen)

It is suggested to AVOID:

- Refined grains such as white flour or white rice, wheat flour, barley, oat, spelt, rye, etc.
- Refined sweeteners such as sugar, any form of corn syrup, cane juice, or the artificial stuff like Splenda, agave, stevia (with the exception of Donna Gates's Body Ecology Stevia—check out her book, *Body Ecology Diet*).
- Deep fried foods
- "Fast foods"

How to Avoid Processed Food in General

Read the ingredients label before buying anything. If what you are buying contains more than five ingredients and includes a lot of unfamiliar, unpronounceable items, you may want to reconsider before buying. Be very particular about what you are eating from a box, bag, can, etc.

Increase your consumption of whole foods especially vegetables and fruits. Try to avoid obsessing over the calorie and fat content. We are not saying dismiss it completely, just don't obsess about counting calories, fat grams, or carbs. All calories are not created equally! When your only concern is selecting whole foods that are more a product of nature than a product of industry, then you are on the right track.

Buy your bread from a local bakery. If you find yourself in Florida, check out Joey's Bakery in Boynton Beach. They have gluten free, vegan and paleo options. They also will ship to any state if you do not have a local gluten- free bakery. For pasta, we like Tolerant, TruRoots, Felicia Organic, and Jovial gluten-free pasta.

And it may be tempting, Mama, but avoid ordering off the kids' menu. Most often things like pre-made chicken nuggets, fries, and pasta are made with white flour and corn flour, among other things. The next time your family is out to dinner, try selecting from the main menu. Consider assembling some sort of side-item plate (like baked sweet potatoes, steamed veggies, grilled chicken, and whatever else your kid will benefit from) and/or try sharing some of your meal.

Visit your local farmer's market the next time you need to restock your fridge. Not only will you find food that is in season, which is usually when it is most nutritious, but you will also find a selection of pesticide-free produce and locally grown fruits and veggies.

Disclaimer: try not to become obsessed or paranoid, just make wise decisions and use your intuition. No one eats perfectly all the time. That is why our detox systems are in place—to help us eliminate the bad stuff. But, when we are constantly overwhelming our bodies with synthetic, man-made crap, that is where the problem lies. The point is that we're empowering ourselves by understanding what's healthy and what's not, as opposed to just blindly following the herd. We think it's perfectly healthy to break the "rules" every once in a while. When you are too strict it feels like you're being deprived and you're setting yourself up for failure and self-sabotage. Baby steps.

Healthy Eating is not Just About Healthy Food

By Lindsay

I learned early on that my responsibility as a parent is not to make my children eat food but to provide healthy food for them at every meal. I don't ever force them to eat the meals. They know they will probably not be getting anything else so they usually eat. But sometimes they don't, and I don't make that a big deal for them or me. I want it to be their choice and never feel forced to eat. It's natural in their growth process to have times when they eat a lot and other times when they eat little. I see it as totally natural and don't let myself stress about it.

The greatest thing I want to teach my children is to enjoy food. To let it fill their bodies and to feel good about it. My hope is that preparing and eating food can be something they can enjoy together in community for the rest of their lives.

I also aim to model for them how important our bodies are—and that we need to fill them with good things because our health is essential. It has a great impact on our mood and attitude and energy level. In keeping up our vitality, we need to eat well.

Having children is a blessing in that we choose to eat better because we want our children to be exposed to good things too. It also means not to get too caught up in all the information out there and trust ourselves and what we can do for our family. Not to let them see food as anything other than what it is: nourishment, not comfort, or guilt, just nourishment.

The Practice

The greatest thing when it comes to health is what goes along with it: our mindset about our bodies, our food and the community act of eating and enjoying food. Here are a handful of practices that will help you embrace a Peaceful Mama Mindset.

- **Love your body as it is.** You have a woman's body, Mama, not a girl's. Feel fit and strong and whole in your body. Let the MAMAHH Moments bring strength and synergy to your body, mind, and spirit. When you like who you are, it radiates outside of you. You feel better about yourself and the life you are living. And in turn, you choose to eat better and desire to move your body to make it stay strong. With our children learning everything by what we model, it's a good time to challenge any false beliefs we have and make sure we are feeling good about our health.

- **Make meals fun.** Let them be something you do in community together, and turn them into a positive experience. Family meals can be a ritual in your home, and with intention it can continue even as your children's activities and social lives become more busy. Family mealtimes are important for children. You can talk about a lot of things around health as well as life at the table so that it remains a cherished time for all.

- **Combine gratitudes with mealtime.** Start a tradition of everyone saying something they are grateful for at dinner. At Lindsay's house, you'll hear her family say this prayer: "Thank you for the food we eat, thank you for the world so sweet. Thank you for the birds that sing. Thank you God for everything." Sharing what you're grateful for or naming your favorite part of the day is simple and a sure way to count everybody's blessings—and they add up!

- **Prepare meals together when possible.** Sometimes you need to prepare dinner alone, which can turn into solo play time for the kids. But other times, it is nourishing to prepare food together, and it's fun too. Your children will learn how to prepare their own meals—what a gift.

- **Food shop together.** Letting your little ones help choose the produce and snack foods makes them feel part of the process of making the meal—and by extension, we find they are much more likely to try new things and eat more of the food that's good for them.

REFLECTION TIME

OK, Mama, it's check-in time! But before we ask you a few soul-searching questions about your relationship with food, we'd like to make one thing perfectly clear. First and foremost, we strongly believe that every person's body is very different and can benefit from and properly digest certain foods better than others. Which basically means, we wouldn't say, "Everyone should eat three to four servings a day of fruit, four to five servings of vegetables, four servings of protein and five to seven servings of carbs." We would feel irresponsible and be doing you a disservice if we generalized nutrition in that way. We all have different blood types and ancestry; we are all at different stages in our lives and have various inflammatory responses to foods; and we have different genetic make-ups and diseases or potential issues that could arise, etc. Therefore, we are not able to responsibly suggest a strict menu plan for everyone to follow.

With that being said, there are some things that everyone should avoid. Regardless of genes, blood type, age or gender, no one should eat poison, right? Well, through our education, research and experience, we believe gluten is like a poison. For some people, it is a very slow-acting poison that doesn't present itself until the seventh or eighth decade of life, sometimes as Alzheimer's. And, for others it is a quick-reacting poison which immediately screams Celiac. And, then there is the in-between, which can manifest as bloating, gas, eczema, cradle cap, chronic congestion, itchy face, brain fog, headaches, migraines, severe acne, fatigue, muscular disturbances, bone and joint pain, etc. This is a long list of symptoms that people generally treat with a pill or a cream, not even considering that removing gluten could also remove the reaction. We are so accustomed to quick fixes—but, taking a pill is like putting a towel on the floor when there is a flood. Do you want to continue putting towels down or do you want to turn off the faucet?

Here are some questions to ask yourself to help you be true to yourself in your relationship with food. Reflection Time is focused here because of its profound impact on your health.

- What do you generally eat for breakfast, lunch, dinner and snacks? What about when you go out for a date night?

- Is the majority of what you are consuming processed, packaged foods, or are you eating organic, real, whole foods?

- Are you eating lots of breads/pastas? Baked goods? If so, can you improve the quality of the foods you are consuming? Have you added some of our suggestions to your grocery list yet?

- Do you eat canned and/or frozen foods? If so, why? Are your reasons tied to cost and convenience, and how would it feel to experiment with changing your approach? And are you making sure that any canned foods come in BPA-free packaging?

- Are you shopping around the perimeter of the grocery store (where the produce tends to be) or do you spend most of your time and money on "food" purchased in the aisles? What new and wholesome products can you find along the perimeter next time?

- When was the last time you read a food label and looked at the ingredients before checking out the fat and calories?

Ideally you would:

- Eat organic, real, whole foods as opposed to packaged foods.

- Eat gluten-free breads/pastas and baked goods with high-quality ingredients (not potato, soy, corn, tapioca, etc.)

- Minimize the amount of canned and/or frozen foods (organic preferable).

- Encourage yourself to buy mostly from the perimeter of the grocery store, meaning from the produce and refrigerated sections where the food is fresh.

- Learn how to properly read a food label (i.e., look at ingredients versus fat/calorie/carb content).

"First and foremost, we strongly believe that every person's body is very different and can benefit from and properly digest certain foods better than others. ...

With that being said, there are some things that everyone should avoid. ...

We are so accustomed to quick fixes—but, taking a pill is like putting a towel on the floor when there is a flood.

Do you want to continue putting towels down or do you want to turn off the faucet?"

~Natalie

THE EXPERT EXCERPTS
A NATUROPATH'S DEFINITION OF HEALTH

By Judith Thompson, ND

I think of health as a holistic approach to life focusing on physical, mental, emotional and spiritual well-being. Lately, I've also started to view additional components such as financial, social and work health as important to overall well-being because of how they affect our lives. Our relationships with family, friends, communities and finances affect how well we feel, or not. A complete life has multiple prongs and all of them need attention.

Physical health refers to our ability to take care of ourselves, to nourish our bodies with alive food that is organic and free of toxins. It means having sufficient minerals, vitamins and antioxidants to keep our cellular functions optimal. This also includes exercise. Movement is individual to every person. Different types of exercises are suited for different people. Some people do better with vigorous exercise while others do better with calming exercises. My favorites usually involve spending time outdoors in nature to garner its healing aspects of fresh air and sun.

Mental health is the ability to have peace of mind and knowing how to manage stress. Recently, I've started looking at stress as a positive challenge. Some researchers are showing that our perspective on the events in our lives dictate how our bodies will react to stress. It can either have positive or negative effects on our physical body. If we view stress as a challenge to meet or overcome and we psych ourselves up for it, we have positive benefits on the body such as better blood sugar response, improved heart function and clear thinking. If we see it as a burden, then our bodies react negatively by breaking down cellular function, decreasing heart function and increasing anxiety.

Emotional health is the ability to have a wide range of emotions, being able to both express them and come to conflict resolution when our emotions disagree with the emotions of others. Emotional expression is what adds color to our lives and expressing them adds brightness.

Spiritual health is not about believing in religious dogma but more about following the wisdom of our hearts, the ability to let our spirit shine, to let our creativity soar into new dimensions and to allow our spirit the freedom to dream. This can manifest in different ways for people through art, music, writing, travel or spiritual expression.

Financial health has come into the picture because it can affect how well people feel or how easily they can succumb to disease. When people have strong financial foundations, they are free to pursue their dreams. This results in a sense of personal freedom and physical abundance that allows for improved health.

Social health is our ability to get along with others—this means all the people we interact with, whether it's friends, family, people at work or neighbors in our communities. Having positive social interactions can either add to or take away from our health. Having a sense of belonging is another component that increases a person's health, along with the desire to contribute to their communities in a positive way. Positive relationships can enhance the sense of belonging.

Work health. I call it work but it's really about a sense of personal fulfillment. This is about how much people enjoy the activities they do throughout the day. It's important because people spend numerous hours of their day at work. Being involved in projects or events that people care about gives them a sense of accomplishment. It adds to a greater goal of being engaged in meaningful work. Meaning and personal fulfillment contribute to better health while its lack can contribute to ailing health.

Judith Thompson, ND, is a naturopathic doctor with a focus on women's and children's health, and she is co-author of the *The Unvaccinated Child: A Treatment Guide for Parents and Caregivers.* Trained in nutrition, homeopathy, herbal medicine and bioenergetics at the National University of Natural Medicine in Portland, Oregon, her practice combines naturopathic philosophy, modern research and traditional models of care to attain a person's highest level of well-being. Having practiced as a naturopathic midwife, she ignites conscious attention to all levels of well-being for mothers, newborns and children through all stages of development.

A MAMA-R.N. WEIGHS IN ON WHAT MATTERS

By Mary Lynn Snow, BSN, RN

Health is important to new moms for so many reasons. For instance, when you eat healthy and drink enough water, you are fueling your body so you can be more energized and balanced to care for your baby. Exercise is important as well, even if you put the baby in the carrier and walk around the block. Getting your heart rate up and releasing endorphins help you to be a happier person and feel good about yourself. Keeping in touch with other moms or friends who can support you is essential as well. Having someone to vent to and hear that you are not the only mom who has a baby who is up ALL night long, and brainstorming new things to try to combat it, is comforting and helps you feel supported through some rough times. Your mental and physical health are vital in being the best mom you can. It is vital in being able to love and cherish the child(ren) you have brought into this world with your whole heart.

When I had my first child I didn't know how to take care of myself. The only person in the world I wanted to take care of was my newborn son. I would forsake everything to make sure that he didn't need to be with anyone else other than me (even my husband). This was such a detriment to me and I had no idea at the time. Then I had my second child, which made it even harder to see that taking care of me was important. I was burnt out and tired. I didn't like who I was anymore because I'd lost my identity. I was working as a nurse and I love my profession but I only saw myself as Connor and Lily's mom. I didn't see that not taking care of myself was actually a detriment to my kids because I wasn't being the best mother I could be. I was in a dark place when I realized how necessary it was to take time for me. When my second child was about a year old, I finally got up the courage to join a local gym. That gym membership helped to fuel my mind, body and spirit. I started with yoga classes and advanced to weightlifting and mixed martial arts. I met people, exercised, and learned how important it was to put me first, even if only for an hour a day, a few days a week. I started feeling better about myself, making genuine connections with people outside of my husband and co-workers, and realizing that my kids were OK without me for a little while. So my best piece of advice to new moms is don't wait until your second, third, or fourth child to realize how important it is to take some time for yourself!

Mary Lynn Snow, BSN, RN, and her husband, Ryan, are raising three amazing children together, Connor, Lily, and Harrison. She works full-time as a Nurse Manager at a local hospital. Mary Lynn grew up outside of Boston and resides in the Seacoast area of New Hampshire. She enjoys spending time with her family, traveling, stand up paddle boarding, and working out in her free time.

THE BREAST CRAWL

By P. Fadwah Halaby, CNM

It wasn't until after I'd had my own six children at home and was studying for my nurse midwife degree that I learned about a well-kept secret about newborn babies: the breast crawl.

The breast crawl is a newborn's innate ability to find, crawl, root and suckle on a Mama's nipple within the first hour of life. When a baby is placed directly onto the Mama after delivery, he or she has incredible natural instincts and a variety of sensory, central, motor and neuro-endocrine components helping the babe's little body move and activate its survival skills. Food is part of survival. And, for babies, the breast is where its food comes from.

There have been several studies done on newborns and their ability to navigate their way to Mama's breast. It was first discovered and documented in Karolinska Institute in Sweden in 1987. In this study, twenty-one babies were monitored after birth—and twenty of them successfully completed the breast crawl. The one baby who did not "complete the breast crawl" reached the nipple but needed help attaching. Isn't that awesome?! Of course, this concept has been around for centuries, but only recently discussed, made relatively "mainstream" and formally studied. There are actually nine distinct actions that every newborn will move through if left undisturbed on the Mama's belly—it starts with a birth cry and ends with self-attachment at the breast. It can take an hour or two to complete and can be done any time in the first few days after birth.

P. Fadwah Halaby, CNM (Certified Nurse Midwife) is a home-birthing specialist and the founder of Midwife360 in South Florida, where she previously assisted more than 1,600 women to give birth in hospitals. Fadwah has given birth six times at home and raised five more children over the years through her rich blended-family lifestyle. She and her team of midwives and doulas are dedicated to empowering women to birth in their chosen setting with grace and beauty, and to supporting not only childbirth but conscious conception and pregnancy and the birth of new mothers as well. Holistic office gynecology also provided.

NATALIE'S REFLECTIONS ON THE BREAST CRAWL

I specifically remember a *distinctive* smell postpartum, like I had not showered in weeks, despite my showering multiple times a day. I also remember how large and dark my nipples became. I realize now that my scent was strong so the baby could smell me and it was a distinctive smell not to be confused with a nurse, doula or grandma. A newborn does not have the ability to see clearly when its born. Which is exactly why my nipples became larger and darker. It was so my newborn could find them on his own. Not that I particularly enjoyed these drastic changes to my body then, but now I at least understand why!

When I take a step back and can appreciate the miraculous-ness that we are (pregnancy, delivery, newborn-isms, etc.), I am in complete awe of how little actual thinking/reading and analyzing is necessary. So much of what we "need" to know about Mamahood is already ingrained in us and imprinted into our DNA from our ancestors and their life experiences. Sometimes it's nice to be reminded that we don't have to know everything in our heads, because our bodies and our beings already know exactly what to do. So cool!

How to Thrive in "Mommy Bootcamp"

By Taina Rodriguez, AP

I called the first six weeks after childbirth "Mommy Bootcamp." It is definitely the hardest, most sleep-deprived time of your life, unless you suffer from insomnia. All babies will be on a two-hour clock. Find your baby's rhythm and organize your life around it.

- When they're sleeping, you sleep.

- When they're playing, you find some time to play.

- When they're sleeping again, maybe this time you get around to cleaning and house chores.

- Write it down on a piece of paper and watch as it evolves, but make sure that you're making time for yourself as well.

The more you realize that you've got this and are relaxed, rested and well fed, the more likely you are going to be able to meet your baby's needs. At this time, they really need you and they really need you to be healthy, too.

Health means to me that I feel whole in my body, inspired and hopeful in my mind and Spirit. That I don't have any symptoms or a red flag saying that something needs my immediate attention to be fixed or re-balanced. That I can just relax fully into who I am. Without health, it is really hard to enjoy life to its fullest. My health practice is healthy food, healthy thoughts, healthy words, healthy relationships and healthy actions. Nobody is perfect, including me, but I do make it a point to try and be my best friend, pump myself up when I feel down, look for answers when there is a problem, and have hope.

Taina Rodriguez, AP, is a licensed acupuncturist, herbalist, and massage therapist who specializes in pain relief, stress relief, women's reproductive health, digestive health, and anti-aging. Based in South Florida, her practice combines the best of nature, science, TCM, intuition and years of experience into individualized holistic treatment plans.

Healthy Mama, Know Thyself

By Nafsya Parpia, ND

When I first became a new mom, I was very much aware of my life and internal state before giving birth. I looked back at my life and wondered what exactly would change now that I had become a mom. I feared losing a sense of my own freedom, and also knew that I would re-define what that meant. I decided that it was a sudden time of self re-invention. I had no choice but to examine my life before I became a mom, and then decide what areas of health (physical, mental, spiritual) I wanted to weave in to my new and unpredictable world.

It is important to note that such things will be different for each individual woman. What was key to me may or may not be to another woman. The take-home message is that it is important for new moms to know what it is that they wish to maintain and create in their lives after they have a child.

Particularly, it is critical to have a sense of self—how one wishes to nourish their being (physical, emotional, spiritual) and as well contribute to the world. When a woman has a strong sense of self, she has more to give to her child. It is important that women regard themselves first as their own being and therefore cultivate a sense of self-love.

We as women, are so much to so many—mother, wife/partner, lover, daughter, sister, friend, aunt, grandmother. It is easy for a woman to lose her self-identity in the many important roles that she plays. I have witnessed this happen many times in the lives of both friends and patients. In such a state there can come about a sense of internal loss or lack of fulfillment and therefore great sadness.

Take the time to know what defines your state of health, and then make a plan as to how to create and maintain that in your new busy life, and your new definition of Self as it relates to you being a mother. Through this path, you will find more internal stability and therefore greater joy in your life as a whole.

Nafysa Parpia, ND, specializes in the treatment of Lyme disease and other complex chronic illnesses such as autoimmunity, mold toxicity, environmental toxicity and gastrointestinal disorders. Her practice is in the San Francisco Bay area. Functional and integrative medicine that is heart-centered guides how she treats her patients. Biochemical imbalances, epigenetic expression, toxin exposure, microbial exposure and emotional imbalance are often key in unraveling the mystery of and treating chronic illness. Each of these aspects is different for each patient. With compassionate listening and cutting-edge laboratory tests, she creates treatment plans that are highly individualistic and healing.

WISDOM OF A MAMA-HOMEOPATH

By Svea Block

The thing that saved me...babywearing! I did everything with my baby in a carrier. Those first few months are meant to be the "fourth trimester" where we keep our babies attached, so it was a win-win for both of us. I cooked and cleaned with my baby in a sling. I even meditated while she slept on me. I often danced her to sleep listening to music that I love. I wish I knew it really does get easier. Those first months are so precious but can be really challenging. You're possibly the most sleep-deprived you've ever been in your whole life, you have a sweet, delicate baby who depends on you, and you have to manage to still take care of yourself. Make a list of the things you have to accomplish that day (don't get too crazy) and make sure the list includes self-care too! My list for the day is something like this: brush teeth in the morning and at night, drink 50 ounces of water, take one nap with baby, say a prayer before bed, and sit in the sun for ten minutes. It feels really good when I accomplish that whole list (and some days I do not finish everything and that is OK, too). Also, give yourself some Grace. Your house doesn't have to be perfect (even when you have visitors!). Focus on your self-care first and foremost and everything else follows.

Secondly, always listen to your instincts. So many people want to give advice when they see that you have a baby. But your Mama voice and heart is stronger than anything you read or hear. Trust yourself.

> **Svea Block** is a Classical Homeopath, certified Naturopath and birth doula, as well as a practitioner of Arvigo Techniques of Maya Abdominal Therapy® (a.k.a., Mayan Abdominal uterine/fertility massage). She specializes in fertility and women's health, incorporating mind-body healing into each appointment. She's a mama of one amazing person and is based in Montréal, Quebec, Canada.

THE WRAP-UP ON HEALTH

Our health is integral to our well-being. The first step toward improving our health is accepting where we are now. We've done the best we can with the tools we have. Next, we can think about where we want to be. We can make small changes by integrating some of the techniques and tools we've shared. Devoting moments in our day to nourishing our body, mind, and spirit is one of the greatest gifts we can give ourselves and our children. They learn most by what we model. When they see us living healthily and feel the positive energy we emit from this way of living, it can only help them in paving their path toward health, happiness, and well-being.

HEART

You cannot know the depth of love you will feel for your child until you actually become a parent. We hear about it and read stories of how becoming a parent opens up parts of us we didn't even know existed. A love so deep that you feel what they feel. It's like no other. It's all true. They really do pull at your heartstrings in a way I can't even put into words. I realize that may sound so cliché, but it really is true.

What you don't hear as much but is also very true is how immensely difficult and challenging and impossible it will feel sometimes to love our children. They challenge us in ways we couldn't even imagine—physically, mentally, and emotionally. In the early months, we are stretched beyond belief to care for our babies and meet their needs around the clock. As they grow into toddlers, their impulsive, demanding, downright illogical behavior tests us. Preschoolers, or "threenagers" as they have warmly been called, develop an attitude that surprises you and gives you a brief glimpse into what the teenage years will yield. Something I can only imagine as they get older.

Yet, it's that deep love that gets us through these challenges. As they grow, so do we. The experience of having children is too great to let the challenges outweigh the joy. We know the greatest things don't come easy. We grow to appreciate and value the tough things because they are the most meaningful. Parenting is one of these things—it's the pinnacle of these experiences.

There is something that helps you get through all of these challenges with more ease and calm. That is *surrendering yourself to it*. That doesn't mean losing yourself. It just means losing that part of yourself, the old storyline, that no longer serves you.

THE FACTS

There is a part of us that we depend on too much in our world that doesn't serve us at all in parenting—the ego or critic or negative voice. It's the voice within you that is against you. It has strong likes and dislikes and expectations and judgments. It's difficult to even talk about the ego as part of "The Facts" because of its illusory nature yet enlightening books, such as *The Power of Now* by Eckhart Tolle and *The Untethered Soul* by Michael Singer, discuss the ego in a-matter-of-fact, practical ways that guide the reader toward transcending the inner critic.

When we let go to something greater, we become aware of something within us that is deeper. We know what it is because we feel it. It's heart or love or light or positivity or grace or God. It's within us and connected to a larger, more forceful energy that is pulling everything in our world along. It's life itself. We don't have control of it. We like to think we do and we expend a lot of effort trying to control it. Parenting is something that brings that right back into perspective, though.

Starting with conception. Many of us have an idea of when we want to conceive. It's like a switch. There comes a time when we feel like we're ready. Everything is lined up in our life and we decide that it's the perfect time to have a baby. But it doesn't work that way. There is a plan and flow to our life that is a part of life as a whole. We are all connected to it and it moves us along and brings us exactly what we need. The thing is, it doesn't always look like we think it will look and seems to come when we least expect it. This is hard for us. Especially now that we are used to getting things fast. Information, things, connecting is at our fingertips. We can do everything we want very quickly these days. We think that instant gratification applies to parenting too.

From the moment of conception, we are called to let go to something greater. *That is surrender.* The idea of surrender will also help us when we are trying to conceive, throughout our pregnancy, and most definitely as we become parents and our world changes forever.

The Practice

Even though it's pretty paradoxical to talk about surrendering as a practice (because it actually reflects the ultimate in not doing anything, simply letting go) it is, in effect, a moment-to-moment practice that jives well with the Mindfulness practices we explored earlier in the book.

Surrendering is important because we do lose a part of ourselves when we become mothers. It feels traumatic and we feel all the feelings that come with losing a part of us. For some, this is where postpartum depression comes in. There is a natural sadness whenever we lose something. Once we can let go and see it not as a death of some part of us but instead an awakening to something new, a rebirth of our own self, that is when it all becomes more beautiful and we can flow with our parenting journey instead of against it.

- **Living in Surrender.** We have to let go *to* our children, who are their own beings with their own wills that do not match our own. They are not going to do the things we want when we want them to. They may trick us into thinking that at times—but that isn't the relationship we are meant to have with them. We are meant to be growing ourselves through all the challenging and demanding and also beautiful experiences we have as mothers. We are meant to reclaim the peace that is within ourselves. And, give our children deep loving roots which will enable them to eventually go off into the world and fly.

- **Seeing Our Children as Ourselves.** Our children, through their behavior and experiences, reflect back to us the parts of us that need to grow—all those tender parts that need attention and compassion and love again. We have to be open to this experience and surrender what we thought we knew about ourselves. All of the material physical stuff has to be shed. Our children don't care about that and they won't fit within any mold we have created for them. We are not their parents to mold them into some ideal we've created in our heads. We are meant to give them the freedom, discipline, and openness to feel safe growing into their own selves and following their own dreams. We'll realize early on that we find strength we never knew we had, but it requires us to surrender some of the stuff we've built up over the years that doesn't serve us. We have to let go and it feels scary because it makes us vulnerable to change. But it also feels so good. It's how we are meant to be living: growing and changing every day, evolving into a greater, more conscious version of ourselves. The experiences with our children bring this out of us. It's living from our heart and how we are meant to live.

- **Practicing Mindfulness.** Mindfulness is the powerful and transformative set of attention skills that enable us to be more present. By learning the attention skills such as concentration power, sensory clarity, and equanimity, we become more conscious, aware, and intentional, which leads to more meaning and purpose. As we bring awareness to thinking about the past and the future instead of right now, we start connecting within, to our deeper soul self, and to that of our children. The practice of mindfulness can radically transform your life—leading to better health, greater productivity, performance, purpose, creativity, and stronger relationships, especially with our children.

- **Trusting Our Inner Voice.** When we are living from the heart, we are trusting an inner truth within us that has all the answers. *It's our intuition.* We've all had the many experiences as a mom of looking toward others for what is best for our children. We may even let our worries about our perceived opinions of others take away from giving our children what they really need in any moment— loving acceptance and kindness. It comes from within. We'll never find it outside of ourselves.

- **Loving and Accepting Ourselves.** Giving our children the loving kindness and acceptance they need must come from our own loving kindness and acceptance of ourselves. We can't give what we don't have. That means we must practice mindfulness and pay attention to the way we are talking to ourselves, our inner monologue. Is it positive or negative? Our children feel it too. They are so intuitive. And that energy doesn't raise them up. It negatively impacts their own ability to be calm and free.

- **Choosing Compassion When Difficult Emotions Surface.** You know the way you treat a friend when she is going through a tough time? We need to extend that same level of compassion to our own self. When we are feeling that love within us, we can then give our children that same loving kindness. It is all they want from us. Yes, they need safety, nourishment, clothing and shelter, but love is just as essential. They need that feeling of belonging and being loved, and we are unable to give that to our children when we are lacking self-love and self-compassion.

- **Understanding and Appreciating Ourselves.** We have to know what fills us up and prioritize that into our day as moms. It's too easy to put ourselves last. There are amazing resources out there if you don't even know where to begin with self-care. Some of us have been giving so much of ourselves for others, we don't even know what brings us joy or how to care for ourselves in a way so we are showing up as our highest version. Check out *Get a PhD in You* by Julie Reisler, one of our Peaceful Mama Experts. Taking time to fully understand and appreciate ourselves is important. She guides you through this in an amazing and inspiring way. Showing up as the highest version of ourselves starts with knowing what fills us up.

"Check out the book Get a PhD in You *by Julie Reisler, one of our Peaceful Mama Experts. Taking time to fully understand and appreciate ourselves is important. ... Showing up as the highest version of ourselves starts with knowing what fills us up."*

~Natalie & Lindsay

There are many ways we can fill ourselves up and we've talked about many of them within this entire MAMAHH Moments chapter. All of these pieces are key to feeling loved.

When we feel love within we can give more love out, especially to our families. Sometimes the ones we love the most, our families, are the last to receive our love. Too many unimportant things get in the way and we have nothing else to give. When we take the time to think about what brings us joy and what is the most important to us, we can re-prioritize and refocus so we make time for what is most meaningful. When children know they are loved by the people who mean the most to them, their parents, they thrive in our world. They better handle the challenges that come up, they treat others well, and continue growing and evolving so they can know what their true gift is and bring it into the world. It's what our world needs.

Reflection Time

Grab a journal, Mama! It's time for some heart-opening reflection. These prompts are all about supporting you in the act of surrendering to another way of living—from your heart instead of your head. *(Note: These are not one-time questions with only one answer. You can return to them again and again.)*

- From as early as we remember, we are planted with thoughts and expectations of how we should be. It came from our parents, form our culture, all sorts of outside influences. We have to let go of all of that. *Which expectations have your children brought into the light of your awareness? Which ones are you ready to let go of now?*

- When we tune into ourselves, we are guided toward a way of living that gives us the freedom, fulfillment, and purpose we desire. It comes from something greater though, much greater than our own self. From something that enables us to grow into who we are, that makes seasons change and the world spin. We are no different than nature. There is a natural way and order to our lives and if we can listen to that voice that guides us and move according to our greater plan here we'll feel at peace. It's different from every other person's path and it's as unique and beautiful as we are. Take some time to journal about your unique path. *What little steps can you take today to make sure you are living in alignment with it?*

- Surrender requires all our strength to follow something we do not see or understand but we feel. Surrendering is hard because it doesn't give us clarity on where we are headed. But, we have clarity in that we no longer let our own reactive nature take the lead. We are no longer letting our expectations of what should be or our perceived likes and dislikes that come from our ego self and aren't true to our heartfelt center take over. The clarity comes in a trust that we are being guided by something much greater, a force—it's life or universe or spirit or love. *Simply write about a moment in your life when you felt this kind of clarity—really let the words flow.*

- We let go of our personal reactions and conditioning from our past that plagues us from being present with non-judgmental acceptance and love. *What would you be doing if you weren't being influenced by the reactions of like or dislike?*

Following this deeper guidance—the kind that shows up in your journal—will feel most natural once you take the first step. The first step of anything is scary. But each step after gets easier. By leading with heart, it will take your life in a very different direction from where you thought you wanted to be. But, it will be greater, brighter and more fulfilling than you could have imagined on your own.

The Expert Excerpts
The Wonder of Self-Care

By Diana Shea

My motto has long been "A Happy Mama is a Happy Home." I pour a lot of love and energy into my kids, yet the number one thing I can do to show my love for them is to make sure that I keep up with my self-care. For me, that means eating well, getting plenty of sleep, and exercising. It also means defining what makes me happy and scheduling those activities to make sure that they happen. This involves meshing with my husband to make sure childcare and other responsibilities are covered in order to free me up to care for myself.

It is very easy to lose sight of self-care, right from the beginning. I urge new moms to use sitz baths and self-massage as a way of initiating a short daily practice of relaxation. I remember when my kids were first born, it seemed like we were in constant triage mode—just taking care of immediate needs and trying to get through the day. As time goes on, we realize that we've just entered a new way of life and while it does get easier in some ways, it is mostly because we adjust and learn to manage the chaos better.

Prioritize your self-care in your day; make sure to get your own needs met.

Sleep when the baby sleeps. Wear the baby when you do household chores. Plan your meals. Read or do computer work while breastfeeding. We try to prepare in advance for the experience of parenting, but we don't know up front what challenges we will face or how we will react in difficult situations. This was unnerving to me. I wanted to study parenting and feel "prepared." Yet, I realize now that as with anything in life, if you approach parenting with good faith, gratitude and humor, things will work out OK no matter what. Sure, it might help if you read a few books in advance. But this is one job that you really learn as you go. I also believe that life is perfect; everyone's path is perfect in the way that it is unfolding for them. And the only thing certain about life is the uncertainty. So it's in that space, between life being both perfect and uncertain, that we must find comfort.

Diana Shea is a certified yoga teacher in Hatha and Prenatal Yoga. She is currently the director of The Yoga Centre in Oak Park, Illinois, where she lives with her husband, their two lively girls and sweet dog, Sasha. Diana is working on her first book, *Say Yes to Yoga,* designed to help people find the motivation and confidence to begin a yoga practice.

There's Nothing Like a Mama's Love

By Stephanie Pierre, AP, DOM

The heart is a container of boundless and infinite love to care for a life and recover from the labors of birthing. Remembering this is the key. When we empty ourselves, as we do in birth, we open ourselves up to receive and channel this precious elixir and medium of the great Heart.

This is vital for new moms because our attention may shift from being into doing. We are no longer receiving because we are filled with ideas of how, when, what if, what to do, and all the silly things in our heads. If this leads to feeling cranky, we must remember to receive and *Seek Ye First!* We are Loved, and we are Love. Life becomes effortless again. As you begin to realign by being in your heart, you invite intuition along too, and the wisdom passed from mother to child, through the generations, awakens within you. Being in your heart means you are always in sync with Nature. Your will is in harmony with the divine will. You are in your flow and with purpose to realize your soul's potential as a child of the Great Mother.

Stephanie Pierre, AP, DOM, is a 5th Dimensional Physician, a mothalova of three bambinos, the founder of Soul Glam, a sensual and magical lifestyle brand. Our songstress stargazer has an exceptionally rare and unique healing style that integrates acupuncture, astrology, aromatherapy and shamanic soul retrieval. Stephanie is based in South Florida.

Speak to Your Baby . . . and Listen

By Sheila Spremulli, B.A., PPNE, BCST, CD(DONA), F-LPN

I worked as an OB nurse at Cleveland's University Hospital for Women in the early '70s when Dr. John K. Kennell began studying the optimal conditions for attachment and bonding. At the time, babies were routinely separated from their mothers after birth, slept in glassed-in nurseries, and were only brought to their mothers for feeding.

Today, newborns are immediately placed skin to skin on their mother's belly as an evidence-based, best practice called Kangaroo Birth Care (KBC). During KBC newborns perform an important developmental task as they inch up their mother's body to find her breast, latch on unaided to the nipple, nurse and nestle into mom's upper chest—following her heartbeat all along the way just like they did in utero.

To welcome your baby into his or her new habitat, parents and grandparents can say what I've learned to say to myself and others:

"I know who you are.": "A unit of consciousness from another sphere."

"I know where you came from.": "You came from the invisible spirit world into this visible physical world."

"I know why you're here.": "Your purpose of life is the fulfillment of consciousness, which means self-realization and God-realization." [15]

Sheila Spremulli, B.A., PPNE, BCST, CD(DONA), F-LPN. In her CHARTres 4 Peace LAByrinth© work, Sheila facilitates labyrinth walks that blend her nursing and birth doula experience with her current work as a Prenatal and Perinatal Psychology Educator to help adults *reconceive* themselves by navigating the psychospiritual shifts in consciousness needed to live sustainably and in peace.

THE WRAP-UP ON HEART

You see, the thing with parenting is we are forced to surrender some of our old life. So, we might as well awaken with awareness and grace rather than kicking and screaming and resisting and avoiding until things happen, we hit a wall or things explode. We can slowly start making choices by practicing MAMAHH Moments. Little choices day-by-day lead to a more enlightened and incredibly more fulfilled way of living and parenting.

We aren't meant to be living on autopilot going through all the motions of life without emotion and feeling and connection to it. Everything shouldn't be certain or predictable or comfortable. We are meant to be living, loving, failing, getting back up, and learning how we can serve others like no one else can. Allowing yourself to live this way is the most courageous, compassionate, and connected version of yourself.

Parenting will call us to let go of what we were, but it doesn't have to be a death—it can be an awakening. We just have to see it that way. This is easier when we treat our body with kindness, keeping it moving and strong so it can be our vessel to move toward our purpose—it must be well. We also have to be affirming goodness in ourselves and others—we have to use our own words to shape our choices toward our intentions and purpose in our life. And we must practice mindfulness so our mind is clear and present—then we are aware of what is, not what we think it is or wish it was, just what is. We also must remember that we are meant to be living with abundance in all areas of our life, not just one or two—all areas. When we are feeling abundance, we are feeling and spreading gratitude, which is only bringing more abundance. This is how we are meant to live. When our body is healthy, we are filling it with good food and thoughts—then we can hear the voice within us, our heart. We can lead with heart in all that we do, our relationships our work, our family life. We are guided toward this unity in our life, when we listen to that voice within us.

It's never too late to start living with our heart, with compassion. Every extra moment of heart-full living is great. We have to trust in ourselves, that we are all doing the best we can, while moving forward and courageously following our own path. Wherever we are on our path is perfect for us and right where we are meant to be.

Too often we let our perceived lacks prevent us from moving forward. For example,

"Many of us try to follow others' paths for a while, thinking it will lead to happiness, but it won't. We have to share our story and allow our authentic self to shine because that is where true beauty is discovered. That's when we start really living and setting an example for our children of what it's like to show up as the highest version of ourselves."

~Natalie & Lindsay

a thought like: "I am already too far behind," is a low vibrational perspective and does not serve us. Instead, adopting the mindset and belief that we are exactly where we are supposed to be at this moment in time, reading this book and personally evolving in our own divine right timing. When that is our perspective, then we can accept, surrender and find serenity, because that is life. The only way we fall "behind" is if we are hiding parts of ourselves, not really living and expressing ourselves. There is no other person on earth with our same experiences and ambitions.

Many of us try to follow others' paths for a while, thinking it will lead to happiness, but it won't. We have to share our story and allow our authentic self to shine because that is where true beauty is discovered. That's when we start really living and setting an example for our children of what it's like to show up as the highest version of ourselves. And, that (truly living) is ever evolving.

"Always be a first-rate version of yourself instead of a second-rate version of someone else."

—Judy Garland

Chapter 7

Flexibility in the Practice

Feeling, Listening, and Trusting Ourselves

We offer the MAMAHH practice as a way for us as mothers to become more centered. When we feel balance within ourselves, we can better handle the ups and downs that naturally arise as parents of young children. Being centered in one area of our life isn't enough. When one area is lacking—say our physical health within our body—the other areas of our life feel that lack even if they seem to be going well. This interconnection of all the parts of our life is why the focus of this practice is not just in our parenting. The focus of this practice is within ourselves. And it is meant to proactively spill over into all important areas of our lives—our relationships, our work, our spirituality, our health, and our parenting. It's all connected because how we do one thing is how we do everything.

A misbelief runs rampant that we aren't meant to feel good and be centered, whole, and at peace. Many of us share the belief that if one area of our life is going well then naturally other areas will feel lack. But this is only true if we believe it to be true. We can slowly change by changing the way we think, and implementing practices such as MAMAHH Moments help us do just that. We are meant to feel whole and well in mind, body, and spirit. When we feel this wholeness, it permeates all areas of our life.

We need to raise the consciousness of our world too. Mothers play an integral role in this important shift that is taking place. We house within our bodies new life. We want to give our children the greatest opportunity toward feeling whole and centered—and feeling peace within themselves—as they go out into the world. Things will come their way that will bring them down. We can't prevent our children from feeling failure and falling. All we can do as parents is model how to get back up when we fall. We have to give them the tools to feel whole inside because that is where all of our strength lies. When they feel whole and connected within, the inevitable tough stuff will give them strength, confidence and credibility to move forward. They need to know the tough stuff only enables us to grow. Having a practice that teaches them how to center themselves and find peace within, regardless of what's going on outside, is what our children need to go out and fulfill their purpose here on Earth. A fabulous book that can help us support our children when they are school-aged and older is *The Miracle Morning for Parents and Families* by Lindsay and Mike McCarthy and Hal Elrod with Honorée Corder. It offers a family-friendly framework to incorporate holistic living principles into an everyday practice for kids and parents.

"Our greatest opportunity to parent our children is to trust the inner voice that guides us. It has every answer. Being at peace with ourselves helps us hear that voice with clarity. As we find that greater peace within by practicing MAMAHH Moments... our children are picking up on this too."

Peace for our children starts within us. We can't give what we don't have. We feel that prioritizing a MAMAHH practice, making it a ritual, and eventually a habit, is one tool to help you become more centered, whole, and at peace. We fall and fail and falter a lot as new moms. It's natural. We need the tools to help bring us back to center and the MAHMAH practice can help with that.

We believe having the ability to call on MAMAHH Moments throughout the day offers endless benefits. As our children grow from infancy they (hopefully) begin sleeping more, allowing you more freedom so you can make time for a set daily practice. This is how we create habits that eventually become ritual, and then a new way of living.

Early on though, in those first few months, any spare moment you can pause to practice one or more of the techniques we offer is a monumental accomplishment. You can use certain daily activities as a trigger toward pausing, taking a moment for yourself, and becoming more aware and present again when you are feeding your baby, or when you are out walking, preparing food, or taking a shower. There are many habitual things we do every day that we can turn into moments of pause and peace within.

The last thing we want to do is make any of us feel guilty about where we are in our life. Our practice always moves us toward feeling whole and centered. Life has a way of its own. We aren't here to control life. We are here to ride with it, to flow.

Flowing with life, instead of against it as we sometimes get stuck doing, is accepting ourselves right where we are, wherever it may be. Becoming a parent helps us learn that more than anything else. We don't control life, our children, or much of anything (aside from our responses, thoughts and actions). The only certainty is the uncertainty of it all. MAMAHH Moments help us accept this truth and blossom into a higher version of ourselves to find more peace in the journey. It's a process. Ups and downs are a natural part of the flow. Guilt and negativity over the ups and downs is not natural; it has no place in our body, mind, or spirit.

It is important to accept the truth that we are all on our path. No two motherhood journeys will be the same, just as no two people on this planet are the same. Each family is as unique as the people who are in it. We cannot expect another person to know how we should parent our child. It comes from within. Comparing ourselves and our journeys serves no one.

Our greatest opportunity to parent our children is to trust the inner voice that guides us. It has every answer. Being at peace with ourselves helps us hear that voice with clarity. As we

"Let MAMAHH, the word you will hear so much in your life, be a trigger for peace. Let it slow you down instead of boil you up. Let that simple word be a trigger toward awareness, toward a pause so you can be present in your mind, body, and spirit as you hear it."

find that greater peace within by practicing MAMAHH Moments throughout our day, our children are picking up on this too. They are learning to look within instead of outside themselves for their fulfillment, their joy, their happiness.

Feeling happiness and joy is in the choices we make moment-by-moment. It's choosing to be awake, alive, and conscious. This is where joy lives. It's in the journey, not the destination. It might be hard to accept that. Most of us have been taught that we need to look outside ourselves to find joy, or that it comes in reaching this or that big milestone. But, we are offering a different point of view. We encourage and invite you to make a shift. Our children are here to help teach us that. Their joy is illuminating. Their inner peace is so bright. They falter too—we all do. However, the difference is that they are able to quickly bounce back after a letdown. Why? Because they honor those feelings of anger, sadness, and fear and they fully feel it. Then they move on. As adults, we have lost that ability to fully feel a broad spectrum of emotions that are natural to being human. We feel like we should push it down. The more we push down instead of feeling what comes our way, the more armor we put up. The more armor on us, the harder it is to feel our own selves and feel all the goodness that is around us. When we keep thinking the old thoughts that make us feel bad (e.g., the storyline of us as the victim, the one who isn't loved, the failure, or insert whatever it is), then we miss out on what's in front of us right now. There is always some goodness. We have to choose to think it, see it, and feel it. If we don't make that choice, we miss it. We don't want to miss the joy being a parent brings us. It's not in the next big milestone—it's right now. It's in really being there at the breakfast table, on the walk to school, in the dinner conversation, or at the park.

Moments are all we really have. Our children create magical moments. Moments we are meant to enjoy. They create challenging and astonishing and horrible moments too. But those are the moments that allow us to grow. When we see it as that—as growing through the tough moments, accepting them as they are—then we move on from them more easily and with more calm. Then we are right there with our children again, feeling joy instead of being caught in resentment, guilt or anger, which again serves no one.

So take this practice as you can. Accept yourself wherever you are as you are reading this. Be kind to yourself. Trust yourself and your ability to do what feels right for you.

Let MAMAHH, the word you will hear so much in your life, be a trigger for peace. Let it slow you down instead of boil you up. Let that simple word be a trigger toward awareness, toward a pause so you can be present in your mind, body, and spirit as you hear it.

Remember that first time you heard the word Mama from your child. If you haven't heard it yet, you soon will. It brings joy to your heart and love to your soul. It is the most beautiful sound. You think you will always love it. However, there will be times when your emotional state will be tested when your child utters that sound. And, as you hear that word throughout your life and are surrounded by various circumstances and feelings, remember you have a choice. How do you want to feel? How do you want to perceive the situation in front of you? It's your choice how you respond, regardless of what's going on around you.

When you are practicing MAMAHH Moments, you are more centered, whole and at peace. You will be able to choose a peaceful response to whatever comes into your experience as a Mama.

It's an important choice because our children are soaking it up. The energy within our homes is important. The love we feel for ourselves emanates from us. We need to have both intention and action to be the person we want to be.

Innately, we all have a similar intention: to be the best parents we can be. We all have the intention to be calm, loving, and kind to our children. We need to follow up that intention with action. The greatest action comes from a place of peace.

Let the MAMAHH practice guide you to feeling at peace within yourself, so you can model inner peace and wholeness to your children, and create more peace in our world, one home at a time.

Chapter 8

Extending the Practice as Our Children Grow

W e trust the MAMAHH practice to take us through all the different stages of motherhood. We know as our children age and go through their different developmental stages, we are called to mother differently. We trust that a goal of peace, centeredness, and wholeness within us is the greatest gift we can give our children at any stage.

When we are at peace, feeling loving kindness for our whole selves—we can treat each of our children and anyone who comes along our path with that same level of acceptance and love. This is how our children learn how to treat others as they go out into the world.

As our children age from babies and preschoolers into school-aged, teens and beyond we look forward to embracing MAMAHH Moments to help center ourselves. So we are better equipped to handle the challenges with more calm. To help us appreciate the everyday moments with more awareness and joy. Our children will eventually grow up and be independent. They are only babies for a short while and are meant to be enjoyed, loved, and honored.

We know the stage we are in now—parenting babies and toddlers—while it is challenging, it is also the most precious and joyful time. We don't want to miss it. We want to be centered enough to soak it up so we look back with tears of gratitude instead of tears of regret.

As we experienced in the early days of first becoming parents, there will be immense joy and also challenges with every stage. We wouldn't have it any other way. Our intention remains the same, to feel peace and love within ourselves and follow our own purpose here, to still live our life while being the best parents we can be. We don't want to lose ourselves in parenting; we want to grow into ourselves and start fulfilling our real purpose here.

When we are living a fulfilled, purposeful life—our children feel the positive energy we exude. In turn, we give our children love, kindness, and hope because we are feeling good inside. With this love within ourselves and our homes, our children can go out and live the lives they are meant to live, to fulfill their own unique purposes. They can show their beautiful self to the world because their vision for themselves wasn't squelched by us; it was embraced and empowered. They can trust that no one else on earth can do it quite like they do because their parents accepted them as they are with compassion and love, without comparison or judgment. They know they are perfect just as they are, neither better nor worse than anybody else. That we are all on our own paths and are meant to be in relationship with and of service to others. They know this because they see us live this way in our homes and with the work we do.

We know that whatever age our children are, when we embody ourselves as Peaceful Mamas, we can fill our homes with love. Then our children are more likely to be at peace within themselves, fulfilling their life mission and treating others with the same love, compassion, and kindness they were given in the homes that built them.

They are a gift to help us grow into who we are meant to be, living a life of purpose and fulfillment. Roots are planted within them during the early stages of life. We want their roots to grow into wings so they too can soar into a life of purpose.

We hope you'll become part of the Peaceful Mama community. We would love for you to join our tribe on Facebook and Instagram @PeacefulMamas, where you will come together with like-hearted and like-spirited Mamas who are here to support and guide you on your Peaceful Mama journey. We are also holding Peaceful Mama Circles, which provide massive value, accountability, and personal development practices. You'll find everything necessary to take your use of the book to the next level, including support for custom-tailoring your MAMAHH Moments practice with live Q&A sessions, a toolbox of resources, downloadable guides, audios and videos, meditations, visualizations, writing prompts, mini yoga classes, and more! It's pretty epic, and we would love your presence with us at:

PeacefulMamas.com

ENDNOTES

1. Hanson, Rick, Ph.D. "Confronting The Negativity Bias." *The Huffington Post.* November 17, 2011. Accessed April 23, 2018. https://www.huffingtonpost.com/ rick-hanson-phd/be-mindful-not-intimidate_b_753646.html.

2. Montessori, Maria and Paul Oswald. *Basic Ideas of Montessori's Educational Theory: Extracts from Maria Montessori's Writings and Teachings.* Oxford: Clio Press, 1997.

3. Kaufman, Brittany Collins. "Are SIDS and colic related? Researchers propose new theory." *Notre Dame News*, news release, November 17, 2016. https://news. nd.edu/news/are-sids-and-colic-related-researchers-propose-new-theory/.

4. *Newsweek* Special Edition. "How Stress Can Affect You and Your Unborn Baby." *Newsweek*, March 22, 2015. http://www.newsweek.com/how-calm-your-anxiety- during-pregnancy-315242.

5. For more information, visit http://holisticibclc.blogspot.com and http://breast- feeding.support/directory/jennifer-tow/.

6. Jaslow, Ryan. "Not Cutting Umbilical Cord Immediately May Boost Baby's Health." CBS News. July 11, 2013. Accessed April 24, 2018. https://www.cbsnews. com/news/not-cutting-umbilical-cord-immediately-may-boost-babys-health/.

7. Suttie, Jill. "How Mindful Parenting Differs From Just Being Mindful." *Mindful,* June 13, 2016. https://mindful.org/mindful-parenting-may-keep-kids-trouble/.

8. Emmons, Robert A. and Michael E. McCullough. "Counting Blessings Versus Burdens: An Experimental Investigation of Gratitude and Subjective Well-Being in Daily Life." *Journal of Personality and Social Psychology* 84, no. 2 (2003): 377.

9. McCraty, Ph.D., Rollin and Doc Childre. "The Grateful Heart: The Psychophysiology of Appreciation." In *The Psychology of Gratitude*, edited by R. A. Emmons and M. E. McCullough, 230-55. New York: Oxford University Press, 2004.

10. Seligman, Martin E. P., Tracy A. Steen, Nansook Park, and Christopher Peterson. "Positive Psychology Progress: Empirical Validation of Interventions." *American Psychologist* 60, no. 5 (2005): 410-21.

11. Shipon, Randolph Wolf. "Gratitude: Effect on Perspectives and Blood Pressure of Inner-City African American Hypertensive Patients." *Dissertation Abstracts International: Section B: The Sciences and Engineering* 68, no. 3-B (2007).

12. Wood, Alex M., S. Joseph, J. Lloyd, S. Atkins. "Gratitude Influences Sleep through the Mechanism of Pre-Sleep Cognitions." *Journal of Psychosomatic Research* 66, no.1 (2009): 43–48.

13. Valley Sleep Center, Phoenix, Arizona. "Can You Correct Your Circadian Rhythm?" Accessed April 24, 2018. http://www.valleysleepcenter.com/can-you-correct-your-circadian-rhythm/.

14. U.S. National Library of Medicine. "Eating right during pregnancy." Last modified October 4, 2016, accessed January 22, 2018. https://www.medlineplus.gov/ency/patientinstructions/000584.htm.

15. Cerelli, K. "Interview: John Chitty: Polarity Therapist, Biodynamic Craniosacral Therapist and Psychotherapist." *Journal of Prenatal and Perinatal Psychology and Health*, 28, no. 2 (2013): 101-117.

For our recommended reading list, visit:

PeacefulMamas.com/reads

ACKNOWLEDGMENTS

It takes a village to raise a child and to publish a book it takes a tribe. We would like to thank all of the beautiful and wise contributors to our book. Our team of Peaceful Mama Experts include our Mindfulness Mavens, Margaret Kachadurian, LCSW, Jessica Killebrew, PsyD, and Sheryl Stoller; our Affirmation Angels, Zeresh Altork, M.Ed., CD, CCE, CLC, Cathy Cassani Adams, LCSW, CPC, CYT, and Julie Reisler; our Movement Gurus, Kathleen Haden and Andrea Riggs; our Abundance Aligners, Michelle Brown, Velvet Chong, RN, and Healing Touch Practitioner, and Tonya Rineer; our Health Specialists, Svea Block, Fadwah Halaby, CNM, Nafysa Parpia, ND, Taina Rodriguez, AP, Mary Lynn Snow, BSN, RN, and Judith Thompson, ND; and our Heart Healers, Stephanie Pierre, AP, DOM, Diana Shea, and Sheila Spremulli B.A., PPNE, BCST, CD(DONA) F–LPN. Your knowledge, expertise and dedication to your passions help to make this book a cherished compilation of collective wisdom. We are so unbelievably grateful for your assisting us in this beautiful co-creation.

We want to give a special thank you to our intelligent, experienced, and soulful publisher, Penelope Love of Citrine Publishing. We met you in divine right timing by way of the Universe and you have been such an incredible guide for us throughout this process. Sometimes words do no justice, and that is the case when we attempt to show you our deepest gratitude. We love you. Thank you for gently holding our hands and for truly acting as our book guardian angel.

We also thank Fiona Saltmarsh for her insight, editing, and sharp set of eyes in the last phase of editing the manuscript.

We would also like to thank Hal Elrod, author of *The Miracle Morning,* and Lindsay and Mike McCarthy, and Honorée Corder, co-authors with Hal of *The Miracle Morning for Parents and Families,* for their inspiration to create our own self-care and personal development practices.

Together we give special thanks to our awe-inspiring contributors Skye Dyer and Brahmanand Don Stapleton, Ph.D. Skye, you are an exceptional woman, Mama, singer, and songwriter. We are sincerely touched by your divine words and shared passion for supporting Mamas around the globe. And, Don, you are an icon in the yoga world and we are truly honored that you are a part of our book. Thank you for expressing yourself with such honesty and grace. Your wisdom comes from a place of personal experience and innate gifts.

And now each of us would like to thank our families and very dear friends who have supported and honored us throughout our lives and our book-writing process.

NATALIE

I believe that we choose our parents and therefore our children choose us. I feel blessed and honored that my children trust me to be their guide and guardian in this lifetime. Likewise, I am so pleased I chose my own parents who are always there for my family and me and continue to love us infinitely and unconditionally.

I would like to also thank my Rotag Sistas—Danny, Marisa, Katy, and Heids—my childhood friends, for always being there for me, even as we individually evolve into our own selves. You have been a constant in my life and are considered family. Thank you for being my shoulders to cry on, my partners in crime, my best friends, and my confidants. Thank you for being true friends, and for showing up as non-judgmental supporters and advocates. You make me laugh like no one can and I am so unbelievably grateful for our sisterhood. I also would like to thank all the Mamas and healers in our Holistic Mothering Group for providing love, support, and intricate knowledge of alternative living and healing. I am also immensely grateful to my Posada Natura warrior family for helping bring Peace back into my life.

As they say, "people come into our lives for a reason, a season or a lifetime." So, I thank you all who have been a part of my journey thus far...and those who are to come.

My dear co-author, Lindsay, thank you for collaborating with me, and for being a light-hearted yet heartfelt passion-project friend. I adore you and am so grateful we met!

And thank you, my family, for your unconditional love, for protecting, supporting and loving me despite my woo-woo ways. A special thanks to my parents, Sibylle and Calvin, for being my biggest cheerleaders and always, ALWAYS believing in me.

To my role model, inspiration and amazing grandmother, Mamy Suzy: although you live far away, I have always felt an incredibly deep bond and connection with you and I am inexplicably grateful to have shared so much joy and so many milestones with you. In my eyes, you are the original Peaceful Mama. Thank you for always making me feel so very special.

Jonah and Skye, Angels of Love and Light, I am humbled and blessed to be your Mama. I thank you, Hashem, Creator, Source, The Universe, my guides, angels and all those who watch over us every single day, for gifting me with your presence.

Your innocence, passion and inner beauty help me show up as the best version of myself. I hope I can always be the Mama you want and need.

Lance, Sage Abraham, soul mate, Journey Man, love of my life: thank you for being my strong mountain, my gentle partner, my beating heart, and my motivator. You make me shine on and inspire me to fully live. I will always love, support and honor you, just as you continue to do for me.

LINDSAY

I thank all those people who have come into my life, even for a moment. Every little connection has helped me evolve to where I am today. I am thankful for all the times I was present enough to listen. I am grateful to be living the life I once dreamed for myself.

And I thank all those people who have stayed in my life longer, who have that much more to teach me. I am grateful for all of you: my family, friends, colleagues, neighbors, and the entire Oak Park community where we have made our home.

To my co-writer Natalie, for your beautiful energy and how you always remind me to trust in the divine right timing of everything. I am so grateful to share this mission with you and to collaborate on something that is dear to both of our hearts.

I am especially grateful for my parents, Marcia and Marty, for modeling a marriage and creating a family life that I strive to create in my own family, one of trust, support, friendship, and most importantly love. I thank my sister Molly for being the greatest supporter of my Peaceful Mama journey—from being the first guest on my podcast and at my first workshops to being a support to me with her listening ear and her open and inviting home. And I cherish my brother Alex, sister-in-law Kelly, and brother-in-law Ryan. You make family fun and I am so grateful you are part of mine.

And for the little loves of my life, Calvin, Lucy, and Paige. You make life so much fun and every day exciting. I am grateful for your creativity, your imagination, your big hearts, and the beautiful way your bright eyes see the world. You have given me the courage to blossom into who I am today and I am so thankful.

I am grateful for my husband, Dan, who sees the love inside me when I can't even see it myself. He understands me, he encourages me, and he has always believed in us, even when it was hard. I am grateful to have you as my companion and teacher. I am thankful for everything you have become and for the Ambrose Family I have joined who taught me the importance of trust.

Finally, thank you to the creator of all, within me and in every person and creation, connecting us all. When I am in alignment, everything makes sense and any-thing is possible. I pray I continue to live openly with the values of truth, courage, and responsibility so I may feel Your love in everyone and express gratitude and joy in everything.

And Peaceful Mama, we thank you! We are over-the-moon excited to share this book with the world. We hope it will bring Peace to every Mama and Mama-to-Be who reads and practices our MAMAHH Moments. We love and honor you!

ABOUT THE AUTHORS

LINDSAY AMBROSE is making everyday moments more meaningful as a woman, wife, and mother of three young children. She incorporates her training in Unified Mindfulness and as a DONA postpartum Doula to lead workshops, serve as a mindfulness and spiritual guide, and host the podcast *EveryDayEveryMom*, life recipes for your mind, heart, and soul. *www.EveryDayEveryMom.com*

NATALIE SAGER (a.k.a. "The Modern Hippie Mama") is a mama of two delicious boys, wife to her best friend, journey man and soul mate, and daughter to two incredibly supportive and caring parents. As an author, speaker, teacher, and meditative Yogini, she is passionate about holistic health, organic living, and honoring the divine. Her mission is to help all beings live in pure health with an abundance of happiness. *www.TheModernHippieMama.com*

PEACEFULMAMAS.COM

23292840R10102

Made in the USA
Columbia, SC
07 August 2018